Encouraging feedback from
impacted by this study:

From a leader in Canada:

This study was very 'people friendly' and each lesson was well thought out and to the point, which allowed our group to discuss some of the 'personal impacts' of each lesson. The study was well-received, encouraging, 'awakening', full of insight and healing.

From a national leader in Bolivia:

I received "Your Identity"...thanks to you...it is formidable...We want to prepare a Seminar for leaders, [when] this study [is] translated into Spanish... the Lord Almighty used it with much power in the hearts!

From a national leader in Egypt:

...thank you for the materials on Relationship [Identity]. These are very beneficial and we are constantly using them..."

From a Leadership Training seminar, Nebraska:

Comments received: It was the best leadership training I've ever attended; This all touched my heart; Clarified His love for me; Scales fell off my eyes; Increased my faith and trust in Him; Refreshed my vision; Taught me to wait/rest in Him and not strive to be perfect, win His love by works. Everyone was greatly blessed!

From a group in New York:

Word pictures like, "my life is a tapestry" have helped me to see that God has already stamped His picture on the fabric of me. The underside may contain loose ends and knots, starts and stops, but the thread continues on — love...The richness of His love is what I've been searching for since childhood! Praise Him for rescuing me!

Although I read through the whole book in one sitting...doing the homework was a journey all in itself...I thought I had dealt with a lot of who

I am as opposed to what I do or how others see me. But God began to do a deeper work in my soul.

The beginning of my transformation started in Chapter 2 with really understanding the names of God…

I have learned that I look at Christ every time I look in the mirror. How dare I think any less of myself when God is crazy about me!

From Texas:
Another problem I have is believing that God really cares a 'hoot' about me…But I want you to know that as I read through this study, God has opened my eyes to what my problem really is…I am just beginning this walk out of hurt and disappointment…but I believe I see what the root of all these problems I have stem from. Not knowing who 'I' am in Christ and just how much He loves me. Now isn't that wild!! I have been a Christian forever and a 'spirit-filled' one at that, and am still not free to just be who God created me to be…how much it has opened my eyes to see what truth really is. I can always blame my problems on someone else…but until I look at the real truth, deliverance doesn't come…thank you for the book.."

From a group in Utah:
One dear lady was saved shortly after attending the group. A pastor's wife was also set free, she had been under condemnation for years. Another lady was set free from a domineering alcoholic mother. Another young woman was set free from thinking she should not have been born. The list goes on and on!

From a leader in South Dakota:
In preparation for teaching "Your Identity" for Leadership Development, this leader shared that as she studied it, she cried through the whole thing. She has been transformed by the study. It is a "multiple gift package from the Lord" containing so much meat, especially in the last 2 chapters. The

Lord brought revelation after revelation to her heart about her past (an abusive, authoritarian father), and has even given her a new name.

From various leaders in the U.S.:
As a leader, I feel I can lead from a more steady/secure place.
[It] zeroed in on so many or our symptoms of brokenness.
I saw areas of hurt that I never realized were there.
[It] helped me to see areas of my life I need to let God work in.

From Pastor Dan Hammer, Sonrise Chapel, Everett, Washington:
For all who want to know their "true identity" in Christ, this book is a must read. As Diane's pastor, I have watched her personal walk of integrity. I say with assurance that reading True Identity *will be a blessing for you.*

True Identity

Diane M. Fink

isaac publishing inc. IPI

True Identity

ISBN: 978-0-9792739-8-8
Printed in the United States of America
©2008 by Aglow International, All rights reserved.
Updated Edition
Original printing 2002

Library of Congress Number: 2008935118

Cover and interior design by Isaac Publishing, Inc.

Unless otherwise noted, all Scripture quotations are from the Holy Bible, New King James Version. Copyright© 1979, 1980, 1982, Thomas Nelson, Inc. Other versions abbreviated as follows: NIV (New International Version), TAB (The Amplified Bible), The Message, The Jerusalem Bible.

Isaac Publishing, Inc.
P.O. 342
Three Rivers, MI 49093
www.isaacpublishing.com

Please direct your inquiries to admin@isaacpublishing.com

Table of Contents

Foreword

Jane Hansen Hoyt, President/CEO, Aglow International

"But who do you say that I am?" (Matthew 16:15). Jesus asks the disciples how they see Him. What is His identity to them?

What a common question we all ask at least inwardly, if not outwardly. Who do you think I am? What we are really doing is searching for a perspective of our identity. We want to know who we are. That need to know is within each of us.

Jesus knew who He was and when the disciple, Simon said, *You are the Christ, the Son of the living God,"* Jesus responded and said, *Blessed are you Simon Bar-Jonah…(*Matthew 16:16-17).

We, too, are blessed when we perceive our own, true, God-fashioned identity. In this profound, personal, and biblical study into the discovery of personal identity, Diane Fink talks about the designer labels we often find on our clothing and possessions. She then makes this great statement: You are a "G.A.O." – a "God Almighty Original." I love that truth! Who we are in the eyes of our Maker is what matters. We bear the label of the Original Designer!

Just as Jesus knew who the Father said He was, He desires that we know who the Father says we are. This is our eternal and only truth.

Diane has been a close and valued friend for many years. From the first time I met her, I sensed the deep treasure of God in her. Diane's true identity was apparent, even when she didn't fully see it. This is a woman who has passed through many waters and walked through the fire only to hear the Lord say, "I have called you by your name. You are Mine!" I know you will love the treasure in this woman's heart even as I continue to.

It is my joy to encourage you to follow Diane as she guides you on this path of truth and into your own personal revelation of *True Identity*.

In 2002, her first work on identity, "Your Identity, God's Self Portrait," was published by Aglow and has been a popular and valuable help to Aglow leaders throughout the world. Now this updated version will reach even more women and men through AIM, the Aglow Institute of Ministry, of which Diane is the Director.

Acknowledgements

Were I to list all those who have significantly "sewn" into my life and the tapestry of my own *True Identity,* it would take another whole book. There are some, however, that I must acknowledge without whom this book would not have happened.

First and foremost, Jesus Christ. From the first day I met You, my life has never been the same. YOU truly are the foundation and beginning place of our identity.

Pastors Dick and Marilyn Williamson. For your wisdom, godly counsel, loving truth, and special friendship. Marilyn, I know you are enjoying the eternal fruit of all your labor while here on earth…and the countless lives you touched. We're grateful for the time we had you with us.

Jane Hansen Hoyt. Heart-to-heart friendships like ours don't come along often in a lifetime. I'm grateful for the love and joys, tears and sorrows, we've shared through the years…for each experience has only served to deepen the bond between us. Friend to confide in. Mentor to learn from…I have watched you lead with grace and wisdom and have gained much. You have enriched my life.

Jennie Newbrough. For encouraging and believing in who I am in Him. Friend. Colleague. Co-laborer in the Kingdom. Your input has been invaluable.

Karen E. Anderson. "Editor of the World"…Editor Extraordinaire! Not only your expertise (of which there is much), but your friendship and love.

Pastor Dan Hammer. Joan Bennett and LTM. Avril Vandermerwe. Bonnie Fretwell. Deena Wilson. Sherry and Pam at Isaac Publishing. I could go on…so many are the gifted, talented, caring, encouraging, special people in my life, whom I value and cherish.

My family. Our four wonderful daughters, from whom I learned a lot. Our grandchildren…the delight and joy of my life.

My husband, Chuck. For your steadfast and unconditional love which allows and enables me to be the person God created me to be. You have sewn into the fabric of my life more than you'll ever know…and for which I am forever grateful.

Introduction

Picture a tapestry...a heavy cloth, woven with decorative designs and pictures, often used as a wall hanging. It is usually a beautiful work of art which you might see hanging in a museum or an art gallery. Intricately designed, artfully and skillfully wrought, it is a highly valued work of embroidery or needlework.

Tapestries date as far back as 1500 BC and are evident in the cultural history of many ancient civilizations including Egypt, Peru, China, Greece, and throughout Europe. The process was quite involved and considerable time was needed to create a tapestry. It began with a painting or drawing on linen or paper, usually by a noted artist, which was then copied by the one weaving the tapestry. Only the best materials were used: fine wool, silk, linen, various kinds and colors of threads. Many of the older tapestries were even woven with gold thread.

> Your identity is the greatest issue that affects your relationships, positively or negatively; with God, spouse, children, relatives, friends, and co-workers.

A Process

God has been in the process of weaving a tapestry since He first spoke, "Let there be light." He has taken great care because His tapestry has divine purpose woven into each strand. Some stitches are worked in bold, vibrant colors with strong, thick yarn. Some are soft, muted shades. Some are pastels, light and fresh.

Some of the needlework is fine, precisely sewn stitches using delicate threads.

Each one of us individually is a part of His tapestry. Corporately, He is weaving us together to create a self-portrait through which He can express Himself to His creation. That is His purpose in the earth: to have a people who will represent His image, His nature, His character, to those who are hurting, broken, lonely, without hope, lost. God's heart is always toward the yet-to-be-redeemed. As we allow His Spirit to do a work of restoration in our lives, we will be better able to express His heart to the world.

As we will see in a later chapter, God is also creating a unique tapestry of each of our personal lives according to the design He had in mind when He created us. Ephesians 2:10 states that...*we are God's workmanship, created in Christ Jesus to do good works, which God prepared in advance for us to do* (NIV). It's as if He began with a clean piece of cloth and imprinted upon it His design (identity) for our lives and proceeded carefully and purposefully to stitch it with His loving hands.

Distortions

The problem is that others have "woven" things into our lives as well – knowingly, or unknowingly – distorting and detracting from God's original design for us. Living from a distorted or damaged identity results in any number of issues ranging from unrealized potential to relational breakdown.

Because our identity directly affects the way we relate to the world in which we live, it is essential that we understand places in us where wounds and hurts have distorted our self-concept. We can be unaware of those areas. But, if we are open to God working in our hearts, He can show us, by the way we respond to life's situations, those places in us that need healing.

He wants to reveal to us HIS design, HIS plan, and HIS purpose for our lives so that we can be the distinctive individuals He created us to be. It has been said that the greatest gift someone can give you is their difference from you. God is a God of diversity... He who made each snowflake different, fashioned you specially and unlike anyone else. Think of how boring a tapestry would be that was made with all the same colors, the same kind of thread, and uniform stitches!

In this study we will look at the issue of identity. So much of our life and relationships flow out of who we believe we are, what we perceive our value to be, and where we see our life is going. You may not give it much thought in the course of your day-to-day life as you go to the office or factory or job site, make doctor appointments, grocery shop, run errands, mow the grass, or shuttle kids to soccer practice. But identity is a subject that affects every aspect of your life. Your identity, or the way you perceive yourself in the context of your world, colors the hopes, dreams, goals, and desires for your life. Your identity is the greatest issue that affects your relationships, positively or negatively, with God, spouse, children, relatives, friends, and co-workers.

A Healthy Self-Concept

Let me give you a simple illustration. If, as a child, you grew up with loving affirmation from your parents, your relationship with God (your heavenly Father) is more likely to be healthier than someone who did not receive that from their family of origin. It's probable that trusting God would come easier for you than for someone who did not receive the security of a parent's love and acceptance.

You might be willing to risk pursuing a career or ministry goal that may seem beyond your reach if you are confident in who you are as a person. Even your relationships with others would tend to be stronger because you would be relating from a place of proper self-perception rather than feeling threatened by relationship.

When I attended a secular seminar on the topic of conflict

resolution, I found it interesting that the first and most important building block to resolving conflict satisfactorily was described as a healthy self-concept. You see, most of us relate to others based on who we believe we are, who we think we should be, or what we think others expect us to be. Relating from a damaged or poor self-concept can result in relational dysfunction and conflict.

As we will see in a later chapter, while it may not be parents alone who help to "weave" a person's identity, the family does play a significant role. That was God's purpose in establishing families: to provide a safe environment in which a child could develop physically, emotionally, and spiritually into the person God designed, thus fulfilling His purpose for his or her life. Unfortunately, those whom God intended to be the teachers, trainers, and nurturers (Deuteronomy 6:7, Proverbs 22:6, Ephesians 6:4), that is, parents, all too often have themselves grown up with an unclear or distorted identity resulting from the dysfunction in their families of origin. But God is greater! He is able to restore all that the enemy has taken (Joel 2:25-27).

Knitted In Love

A wonderful story by Max Lucado poignantly touches this issue of identity within each one of us that is at once so basic and yet so profound. It somehow resonates deep within and speaks to the very core of our being.

"In my closet hangs a sweater that I seldom wear. It is too small. The sleeves are too short, the shoulders too tight. Some of the buttons are missing, and the thread is frazzled. I should throw that sweater away. I have no use for it. I'll never wear it again. Logic says I should clear out the space and get rid of the sweater. That's what logic says. But love won't let me. Something unique about that sweater makes me keep it.

"What is unusual about it? For one thing, it has no label. Nowhere on the garment will you find a tag that reads, 'Made in

Taiwan,' or 'Wash in cold water.' It has no tag because it wasn't made in a factory. It has no label because it wasn't produced on an assembly line. It isn't the product of a nameless employee earning a living. It's the creation of a devoted mother expressing her love.

"That sweater is unique. One of a kind. It can't be replaced. Each strand was chosen with care. Each thread was selected with affection. And though the sweater has lost all of its use, *it has lost none of its value* (italics added). It is valuable not because of its function, but because of its maker. That must have been what the psalmist had in mind when he wrote, 'you knit me together in my mother's womb.'"[1]

Can you relate? Have you ever felt like you've been hanging in a dark closet for longer than you care to remember? Have you ever felt ill fitted to the world in which you live, worn out, or worse, like damaged goods? Have you ever questioned why you are even on this blue orb we call Earth and if there is a purpose in this reality we call life? If so, you have grappled with an area that is the very foundation of who you are: your identity.

1

Original Design

Identity Defined

What do we mean by "identity"? Simply put, it is the way we see ourselves. It is a set of beliefs, conscious or unconscious, we hold to be true about who we are. It is, in a sense, the very fabric of our being.

Webster's Dictionary defines identity as, *the condition or fact of being a specific person or thing; individuality.* The word also has the meaning of being the same as. We refer to twins that are of the same sex and look very much alike as "identical" twins.

The term "phishing" is a relatively new concept and is associated with one of the fastest growing crimes in our high-tech world, namely identity theft. Phishing is a word used to describe a scam involving fraudulent email that lures people into providing confidential information. It always appears to come from a trusted source, when it is actually from an imposter. The email tricks you into supplying private information such as bank account numbers, social security numbers, passwords and ID numbers. Armed with your personal information, the criminal then steals your identity and uses it to access your financial resources and credit cards. The financial loss and damage to a good name can be devastating. We too, face an "imposter" – a spiritual enemy – who wants to steal not only our physical resources, he wants to steal our very God-given identity as image-bearers on the earth.

Another term you are probably familiar with is "identity crisis." Often occurring in adolescence, but not limited to that age group, someone in such a state is uncertain of who they are and where they are going in life. In the case of teens, their uncertainty can stem from the fact that they are in transition to adulthood: no longer children, but not yet fully adults.

An identity crisis can occur in a woman when her children are grown and leave the home. Some call it "empty nest syndrome." Her role as mother seemingly has come to an abrupt end, leaving her to wonder how to relate to her world when everything has changed. Retirement, especially for men, can trigger a loss of identity. The job that defined their lives for many years is no longer there. Husbands or wives can experience an identity crisis when they lose a spouse, particularly after many years of marriage. Widowhood is an entirely unknown identity to the newly bereaved, and difficult to embrace.

While we may go through times when our identity is seemingly shaken or transformed by outward circumstances, the core of who we are, our DNA if you will, does not change. The difficulty is that we don't always know our true identity in the depth of our being. The world and the enemy have so distorted our perception of ourselves that we function out of false beliefs instead of the truth.

Two Elements of Identity

Two components that make up our identity are SECURITY and SIGNIFICANCE. Security has to do with our sense of who we are as individuals stemming from a feeling of acceptance and perceived value or worth.

Security

To feel secure and worthwhile, we must know that we are loved with the kind of love that we cannot earn, and therefore, cannot lose based on our actions. Security is the feeling that comes when someone knows our weaknesses, failures, and sin, but loves us still. It's a place of safety where we can just be real and know that we will be accepted and valued.

It has been said that the greatest single cause of a poor self-concept is the absence of unconditional love. I know of only three persons who can love that way: the Father, the Son, and the Holy Spirit. God's love for you is such that there is not one thing you can do to make Him love you more than He does right this moment. Nor is there anything that can make Him love you less. He loves you without condition.

Significance

Significance is the need to know that your life has meaning, that there is purpose in your existence. Another word for it is destiny. Deep within is a desire to know that your life can have impact, that there is a reason you are here, and that you are adequate to fulfill your purpose. Knowing that you are part of something larger than yourself gives you a sense of purpose and value.

As we will see, an identity that is not founded in God will lead to pursuing significance through what the world has to offer: a prestigious job (or ministry), financial success and the possessions afforded by it, fame, power, etc. The list goes on and on. But once again, there is only one source of true significance – God. As our Creator, He knows the plans and purposes He has for us, and they are good (Jeremiah 29:11). A healthy self-concept, or identity, grows from knowing we are loved and accepted, that we have value, and that our life has meaning and purpose.

> It has been said that the greatest single cause of a poor self-concept is the absence of unconditional love.

Who You Are In Christ

As a believer, your true identity can be expressed through the following verses:

Genesis 1:26

Then God said, "Let Us make man in Our image, according to Our likeness; let them have dominion over the fish of the sea, over the birds of the air, and over the cattle, over all the earth and over every creeping thing that creeps on the earth."

We were HIS idea — made in the image of God Almighty, the Creator of all things!

2 Corinthians 5:17

Therefore, if anyone is in Christ, he is a new creation; old things have passed away; behold, all things have become new.

We get a brand new start when we come to Jesus – the slate is wiped clean!

Ephesians 1:6

...to the praise of the glory of His grace, by which He has made us accepted in the Beloved.

We are accepted by Him, therefore we are acceptable!

2 Corinthians 5:21

For He made Him who knew no sin to be sin for us, that we might become the righteousness of God in Him.

Jesus became who we were so that we could become who He is – the righteousness of God!

John 1:12-13

(12) But as many as received Him, to them He gave the right to become children of God, to those who believe in His name: (13) who were born, not of blood, nor of the will of the flesh, nor of the will of man, but of God.

Children of God – born into His wonderful family!

Romans 8:14-17

(14) For as many as are led by the Spirit of God, these are sons of God. (15) For you did not receive the spirit of bondage again to fear, but you received the Spirit of adoption by whom we cry out, "Abba, Father." (16) The Spirit Himself bears witness with our spirit that we are children of God, (17) and if children, then heirs—heirs of God and joint heirs with Christ, if indeed we suffer with Him, that we may also be glorified together.

Our earthly heritage exchanged for His heavenly heritage!

Familiar scriptures, aren't they? And most of us who are believers would say we know that these verses are true. Yet, as we go through this study, we'll see that what we believe with our minds may not be a true reflection of our heart beliefs which are evidenced through our behavior, emotions, and attitudes.

"Head Knowledge" vs. "Heart Knowledge"

We often give mental assent and are in total agreement with what the Word of God states. However, when it comes to walking it out, the truth we hold in our heart is what will be expressed through our actions. It is the difference between "head knowledge" and "heart knowledge." Head knowledge gives assent to, agrees with, and even desires to live according to the truth of the Word. Heart knowledge, or the deep beliefs we hold to be true, is expressed through our words, actions, emotions, and attitudes (Luke 6:45).

Why is heart knowledge so important to the topic of identity?

The "heart" represents our inner being and is the fountain of all we do (Proverbs 4:23). An example of the difference between head and heart knowledge would be someone who says the words of the sinner's prayer to receive salvation, but continues to live the same as before. That's *mental assent* to the need for salvation. But someone who has seen their need for Jesus deep within, not only says the words, but prays from the *heart*, with a resulting change in the life (Romans 10:9-10).

The New Testament Greek word "ginosko" gives us a better understanding of "heart knowledge." In John 8:32 Jesus states: *And you shall know the truth and the truth shall make you free.* The word translated "know" is the Greek word "ginosko" and it means "the recognition of truth by personal experience."[2] That is much more than just knowing something as a fact. In the case of salvation, it is a personal encounter with the Truth that goes beyond mental understanding to the very depth of the heart. To put it another way: *Such "knowledge" is obtained, not by mere intellectual activity, but by operation of the Holy Spirit consequent upon acceptance of Christ.*[3]

When we enter into a relationship with Jesus Christ through salvation, we open our heart to Him and the Holy Spirit who is then able to bring recognition, understanding, and acceptance of the truth of the Word of God. What is the truth we need to know by experience? It is God's love *for* us, acceptance *of* us, and the value He sees *in* us. We need to know that He has a planned purpose and destiny for our lives.

As He Thinketh...

Why is heart knowledge so important to the topic of identity? Because we are told in Proverbs 23:7, *For as he thinks in his heart, so is he.* Who we are and what we become has much to do with the way we think about ourselves in our heart.

The word translated, *thinks*, means "to split open, reason out, reckon, estimate."[4] It actually comes from a word for "an opening, door or gate."[5] We already defined heart as the inner being. And one final significant word in this verse is so. It means to establish or fix. Putting these definitions together, we understand the verse to say: AS A PERSON REASONS, RECKONS, OR ESTIMATES HIMSELF TO BE IN HIS INNER BEING, SO IT IS ESTABLISHED AND FIXED: THAT IS WHO HE IS!

Closed Door

If you are only open to seeing yourself in one way, the door is closed to perceiving yourself in any other light or truth. If, due to wounding, trauma, neglect, or other damaging experiences, you have perceived yourself as unworthy or inadequate, that is how you define yourself as a person.

Woven into the fabric of your being are heart beliefs and perceptions so deep, that even the Word of God cannot be embraced fully. You heard the lie before you heard the truth, now you hear the truth of God through the lie! But God is able, as you choose to open those places in your heart to Him, to impart to you HIS identity, HIS destiny, HIS plan and purpose for your life.

Let's Talk About It

1.   Share with the group how you would describe your identity. Have experiences from the past affected the way you perceive yourself? Share one or two examples.

2.   What are your heart feelings as you read the verses related to who you are in Christ? Do you think it is more of a mental assent or "heart knowledge" for you at this point in your life?

3.   When have you seen behaviors, emotions, or attitudes that betray what you truly believe about yourself?

4.   Have you personally experienced the truth that you are a child of God? A joint heir with Jesus? The righteousness of God? Share what that means to you.

5.   Do you know "by experience" the kind of love that you cannot earn and therefore, you cannot lose based on your behavior?

 At Home This Week

Meditate on the scriptures in this chapter, looking them up in various translations of the Bible to gain fresh perspective on them. Write out in your own words what they mean to you.

 Truth to Embrace

1.   Two components that make up our identity are security and significance. Security has to do with our sense of who we are as individuals stemming from a feeling of acceptance and perceived value or worth.

2.   Significance is the need to know that your life has meaning, that there is purpose in your existence. Another word for it is destiny.

3.   As a person reasons, reckons, or estimates himself to be in his inner being, so it is established and fixed: that is who he is!

2

What's In A Name?

That which we call a rose by any other name would smell as sweet.
— William Shakespeare

Shakespeare was right. Were we to identify a rose by another name, say daisy or daffodil, it would change neither the beauty nor the sweet fragrance of the flower. It would not change its essence, or identity. We have come to know this family of plants as roses and can identify them easily by some of their characteristics – color, shape, fragrance. When someone says the word "rose," you know exactly what she is referring to.

Names are significant and are very closely associated with identity. Some time ago, an article appeared in a local newspaper[6] about a new direction people are taking in changing their family name, or surname. One couple opted for, "Rain," because they wanted to be identified with their commitment to the environment. Another chose her dog's name as her surname. Yet another couple both kept their family name and decided when they had children, the girls would receive their mom's surname and the boys their dad's. I couldn't help wonder as I was reading, what effect that would have on them as family, or even on the children's individual identities. Rather than being connected to both parents, they were linked to one or the other.

Others interviewed changed their names to break from a pain-

> Names are significant and are very closely associated with identity.

ful past. What effect might changing surnames have on family history and genealogies? Without the ability to trace families through names, entire lineages could be halted. Thankfully, the trend does not appear to be gaining ground. According to the same article, a study showed that 90% of women still take their new husband's name when they marry.

Biblical Names

Names were of great significance in biblical times and were given for a number of different reasons. Sometimes, a child was named because of a certain characteristic. Esau's name means "hairy" which reflected his appearance (Genesis 25:25).

Some names were given to signify a national event in the history of the nation of Israel. 1 Samuel 4:19-22 tells the account of a baby born to Phinehas' wife whom she named, Ichabod. The Philistines had captured the Ark of the Covenant and her husband and father-in-law (Eli) had died. To commemorate the darkness of the time, she named her son Ichabod, which means, *the glory has departed from Israel.*

At times, a name was given to reflect the circumstances of the child's birth or the parent's feeling at the time. Moses was so named because he was *drawn out* of the water. Isaac means *laughter* and expressed his mother's joy at his birth.

Character or Nature

People in the Bible believed there was a vital connection between the name and the person it identified. Therefore the meaning of names was very important because it signified character, nature, and destiny.

Nowhere is this principle more clearly illustrated than in the names referring to God. Throughout Scripture, God was unfolding His nature to His people through word pictures He used to disclose Himself. He was weaving a self-portrait, expressing His identity through His names and His encounters with Israel.

At the burning bush, God revealed Himself to Moses as *I AM WHO I AM* (Exodus 3:14)…eternal, self-existent one.

In Exodus 6:3-4, Moses receives a new revelation of God: *I appeared to Abraham, to Isaac, and to Jacob, as God Almighty, but by My name, LORD, I was not known to them.* LORD, or Jehovah, is the personal name of God as opposed to God Almighty *(El Shaddai)*, which means the all-powerful, self-sufficient God.

> God was unfolding His nature to His people through word pictures.

Jehovah-New Revelation

This new revelation as "Jehovah" expresses the personal, covenant relationship of God to His people. It also signified that now the way was open for the Israelites to know God personally, since Jehovah, or Yahweh, is His name as a person.

We read in Exodus 34:5-7, that the Lord proclaimed His name to Moses by describing His character and attributes: *…merciful and gracious, longsuffering, and abounding in goodness and truth, keeping mercy for thousands, forgiving iniquity and transgression and sin, by no means clearing the guilty…*

God continues to develop the tapestry of His nature and character throughout the Word by means of His names.

The Names of God

Jehovah Tsidkenu
    The Lord our Righteousness   (Jer 23:6, 33:16)
Jehovah M'Kaddesh
    The Lord our Sanctifier   (Ex 31:13)
Jehovah Shalom
    The Lord our Peace   (Judg 6:24)

Jehovah Shammah
> The Lord our Ever-Present One   (Ezek 48:35)

Jehovah Rapha
> The Lord our Healer   (Ex 15:26)

Jehovah Jireh
> The Lord our Provider   (Gen 22:14)

Jehovah Nissi
> The Lord our Banner   (Ex 17:15)

Jehovah Rohi
> The Lord our Shepherd   (Ps 23:1)

There are other word pictures of God's nature as well, but He is seen in His fullness in the person of His Son, Jesus.

He is the sole expression of the glory of God – the Light-being, the out-raying of the divine – and He is the perfect imprint and very image of [God's] nature...(Heb 1:3, Amplified).

For in Him dwells all the fullness of the Godhead bodily (Col 2:9).

Jesus said, He who has seen Me has seen the Father (John 14:9)...

Jesus also states that He has manifested the name of the Father (John 17:6), meaning He has revealed the divine nature of God to men. Jesus' own character was described through Isaiah's prophecy: *And His name will be called, Wonderful, Counselor, Mighty God, Everlasting Father, Prince of Peace.* (Isaiah 9:6).

Authority

Names also denote authority and power. In the New Testament, Jesus instructs us that whatever we ask in His name, that He will do, that the Father may be glorified in the Son. If you ask anything in My name, I will do it (John 14:13-14). And in Mark 16:17-18: *In My name they will cast out demons; they will speak with new tongues; they will take up serpents; and if they drink anything deadly, it will by no means hurt them; they will lay hands on the sick, and they will recover.*

The disciples healed in the authority and power of the name of Jesus (Acts 3:6-7, Acts 4:7-10).

You can see this principle of names representing authority in operation even in the modern workplace. If you were asked to do a project because the CEO of the company requested it, how much more quickly would you get it done than if the receptionist asked you to do it!

Destiny

In the Bible, names were also given to signify the destiny, or purpose of a person. Noah, whose name means, "rest," was destined to bring rest, or comfort, to his family when God's judgment came on the earth in the form of the flood (Genesis 5:29).

Elijah ministered at a time in Israel's history when the king and queen had established the worship of Baal in the land. Elijah's name means, "Jehovah is God." Every time Elijah's name was spoken, it was a declaration of the truth that Jehovah is God in Israel, not Baal!

Jesus' name, too, bespeaks His destiny: And she will bring forth a Son, and you shall call His name JESUS, for He will save His people from their sins (Matthew 1:21).

So we see that names have significance in the Bible for a number of reasons: identifying characteristics, remembering a national event, reflecting the circumstances of birth, or the parent's feelings at the time. But the most meaningful aspect of a name is that it is linked to the very identity of a person: character, nature, and destiny.

Let's Talk About It

1. How have you experienced any of the aspects of God's character represented by His names as listed in this chapter? Are there other names of God you have personally experienced?
2. God is first of all, "Father." Is it easy for you to relate to God as your Father? If so, why? If not, why do you think that is?
3. Can you share about a time when you called on the authority in the name of Jesus? What was the result?

 At Home This Week

Look up some of the names God calls us. (His children, joint heirs with Christ, the Bride of Christ, etc.) Then ask God to anchor them in your heart.

 Truth to Embrace

1. People in the Bible believed there was a vital connection between the name and the person it identified.
2. Names have significance in the Bible for a number of reasons. The names of God reflect His nature and character, His authority and power. Names given individuals signify a person's purpose or destiny.
3. God continues to develop the tapestry of His nature and character throughout the Word by means of His names.

3

A New Name

A Personal Journey

A number of years ago, I was seeking the Lord for greater depth and intimacy in my relationship with Him. God takes us through seasons in our walk with Him when He stirs our hearts with a dissatisfaction and longing for more of Him. There was a hunger in my spirit to know Him more, a crying out for an increase of His presence in my life. So strong was the longing that I lived out of scriptures like Psalm 42:1-2...

As the deer pants for the water brooks,
So pants my soul for You, O God.
My soul thirsts for God,
For the living God.

What I learned was this: when you seek God's face, He'll show you yours.

And Psalm 63:1 (Amplified)...

O God, You are my God; earnestly will I seek You; my inner self thirsts for You, my flesh longs and is faint for You, in a dry and weary land, where no water is.

And Psalm 84:2...

My soul longs, yes, even faints
For the courts of the Lord;
My heart and flesh cry out
For the living God.

I wanted God to reveal to me His ways, as He did to Moses, not just His acts as He did the Israelites (Psalm 103:7). So I began crying out, seeking His face in the secret place where it was just He and I.

One of the things I learned was this: When you seek God's face, He'll show you yours! Over a period of time, I began to realize that what began with my seeking more intimacy with Him actually became an identity journey.

He began to reveal sources in my life that I looked to for my identity, people I turned to in order to define who I was as a person. It was a painful time. You see, I thought I had dealt with many of these issues through the counseling I had received years before. And indeed, I had received much healing.

But in the process of being fashioned into His tapestry, He continually works to cut away and unravel the unlovely stitches that have been sewn into our lives by the enemy, so that He can weave His character and likeness into us. Ultimately, the Lord led me to change my name from a nickname I had used most of my life, to my given name. The significance of this act of obedience was to leave behind the woundedness of the past and embrace my true identity in Christ…the identity He had given me from the beginning.

A Future Hope

A portion of Scripture that came alive to me during this time was Isaiah 62:1-5, 12. The Lord brought revelation on the issue of identity through this passage. Biblical prophecy declares future things in the plan and purposes of God, as in this portion of Isaiah. In effect, it looks ahead to the completed tapestry even though it is still very much a "work in progress." Let's begin with the first three verses of Isaiah 62.

Isaiah 62:1-3
For Zion's sake I will not hold My peace,
And for Jerusalem's sake I will not rest,
Until her righteousness goes forth as brightness,
And her salvation as a lamp that burns.
(2) The Gentiles shall see your righteousness,
And all kings your glory.

*You shall be called by **a new name**, [emphasis added]*
Which the mouth of the LORD will name.
(3) You shall also be a crown of glory
In the hand of the LORD,
And a royal diadem
In the hand of your God.

In this portion of Scripture, Isaiah, through the power of the Holy Spirit, foresees Jerusalem's future identity. Both Israel and Judah had experienced a long period of prosperity and power. Idolatrous pagan worship had become commonplace in Israel.

While Judah had maintained an outward conformity to God's law, inwardly they were falling into moral and spiritual decline.

Much of the book of Isaiah speaks of God's imminent judgment upon the nation for having violated His holy covenant. The prophet could foresee the coming captivity, first of Israel, then Judah. Along with the warning, which was intended to turn them back to obedience to God, Isaiah also lays a foundation of hope and a promise for Israel's future redemption. The opening verses of chapter 62 speak to that hope and promise of restoration.

Destiny for Jerusalem

God, through Isaiah, declares that Israel's righteousness and salvation will be made evident to both Gentiles and all kings. In effect, God is saying that the true identity and destiny He intended for Jerusalem from the beginning will, indeed, come forth.

While the prophetic significance for the nation of Israel as God's chosen people is obvious in this passage, we can make application to the church, as spiritual Jerusalem. As such, this portion of Scripture has much to speak to us concerning our identity, personally and corporately, as we will see in the following chapters.

God will bring forth the church's true identity, just as He will the nation of Israel's. When He does, the other nations will see it and know that He is God!

A New Name

Verse 2 declares the Lord will give Jerusalem a new name...one that will express who she truly is.

God often changed people's names in the Bible.

- Abram became Abraham (Gen 17:1-8, Neh 9:7). Abram means, "exalted father" while Abraham means, "father of a multitude." In changing Abram's name, God was calling forth the greater destiny he had been created for. An "h" was added to Abram's name to make it Abraham. Because "h" is one of the letters of YaHWeH, it is as though God was imparting to him a portion of His own name[7], and hence, a part of His nature.

...a new name speaks of new character, new dignity, new favor, and new destiny

God changed Sarai's name to Sarah, including an "h" in her name as well. Sarai, "Princess," became Sarah, "The Princess," or "Queen," linking her in co-rulership with her husband and including her in the covenant promises (Gen 17:15-16).

Both were being called out of the identity of their past, into a new land with a new identity and destiny in God.

- Jacob means, "deceiver," a picture of his character before he wrestled with God. His name became Israel, "prince," after he struggled and succeeded in receiving God's blessing (Gen 32:27-28; 35:9-15). He was destined to become the head of the 12 tribes of Israel.

- Did you know Moses changed Joshua's name (Numbers 13:16)? It was Hoshea, which means "salvation." Moses changed it to Joshua, "Jehovah is salvation," knowing it would be through Jehovah that the Israelites would conquer Canaan.

- Daniel and his three friends (Hananiah, Mishael, and Azariah) had their names changed by King Nebuchadnezzar's chief eunuch to Belteshazzar, Shadrach, Meshach, and Abed-Nego

(Dan 1:6-7). Their re-naming was an attempt to destroy their identity as Hebrews, establish them as Chaldeans, and turn them away from the God of their fathers. Each of their Hebrew names had something of God in them:

Daniel – *God is my Judge*

Hananiah – *The grace of the Lord*

Mishael – *He that is the strong God*

Azariah – *The Lord is a help*

The Chaldean names all had references to the idols worshipped in Babylon:

Belteshazzar – *Keeper of the hidden treasures of Bel*

Shadrach – *Inspiration of the sun* (which the Chaldeans worshipped)

Meshach – *Of the goddess Shach*

Abed-Nego – *Servant of the shining fire* (which they also worshipped)

The attempt of the Chaldeans to turn them from their true identity was unsuccessful, but the changing of their names was intended to move them away from their Hebrew heritage and religion and towards their "new" identity. Not incidentally, their new identity was as slaves!

This same practice is occurring in our world today. There are reports from the nation of Sudan detailing the abduction of young males for use as slaves by Islamic fundamentalists. To undermine and eradicate, if possible, their Sudanese heritage and identity, they are given Islamic names.

- Esther's Hebrew name was Hadassah, meaning myrtle (Esther 2:7). Myrtle trees have fragrant leaves and starry white blossoms and held spiritual significance for the Israelites as symbols of peace and joy (Zechariah 1:8-11). Esther became a source of peace and joy to her people when, in risking her own life, she saved them from utter destruction. Interestingly, Esther means, "star."

- Jesus changed Simon's name to Peter following his declaration of Jesus as Messiah and Son of the living God (Matthew 16:18). Impulsive, impetuous, unstable Simon is called, Peter, the rock. Can't you just see Jesus smiling as He changes his name, calling forth Peter's true identity and destiny as one of the building stones in the early church? Jesus saw the potential in his disciple and called it forth prophetically through his name.

- Then there is Saul, who became Paul (Acts 13:9). Fitting that the disciple to the Gentiles should be given a Roman name!

The ministry of Aglow has experienced a name change as well. Once known as "Women's Aglow Fellowship," the ministry is now "Aglow International." What began with a small group of women over 40 years ago has grown into a worldwide movement reaching 17 million people annually in over 170 nations. "Aglow International" expressed the increased scope, vision, and reach of this movement.

In all of the instances above, a new name speaks of new character, new dignity, new favor, and new destiny. When God changes a name, it is often to impart a new identity for that which He is about to do in and through the person.

Let's Talk About It

1. What names do you call yourself? (Positive or negative.)
2. What names have you been called that have either been a source of pain or a source of encouragement?
3. Have you or someone you know changed his/her name? What was the significance of it?

At Home This Week

Read the accounts in this chapter of people whose names were changed. Note any insights the Holy Spirit gives you in relation to their character and/or nature before and after the change.

Truth to Embrace

1. An "h" was added to Abram and Sarai to make them, Abraham, and Sarah. Because "h" is one of the letters of YaHWeH, it is as though God imparted to them a portion of His own name.
2. The process of being fashioned into God's tapestry means that He continually works to cut away and unravel the unlovely stitches that have been sewn into our lives by the enemy, so that He can weave His character and likeness in us.

4

Tangled Threads

Have you ever been to an amusement park "fun house"?

One of the things I liked to do as a child was to stand in front of all the strange mirrors that would change your shape in the funniest ways. One mirror would make you look very long and skinny. Another would make you look short and fat. Still another would make your body look like it had waves and curves where you knew there weren't any!

The experiences we have in life can do to our self-perception what the mirrors in the fun house do to our reflection – distort and twist the way we see ourselves.

As we continue in our study of Isaiah 62, we see that Isaiah was describing the distorted identity of Jerusalem, which was actually a result of her turning away from God. The first part of verse 4 states:

Isaiah was describing the distorted identity of Jerusalem, a result of her turning away from God.

You shall no longer be termed Forsaken,
Nor shall your land any more
Be termed Desolate.

Forsaken and desolate. Accurate words to describe her condition during the captivity to Babylon.

What comes to mind when you picture Jerusalem during the siege and subsequent captivity? I think of pictures I have seen from World War II: bombed out cities with nothing left for miles around except piles of bricks and rubble; homes and buildings reduced to smoking heaps, remnants of what once was. I think of empty streets and empty homes, all the people taken away captive.

Perhaps some of you reading this have not only seen pictures, but have lived through the pain of that devastation during World War II, or of national wars such as the Korean War, the Vietnam War, or the Gulf War. The world continues to live through the war on terrorism in the wake of the attacks on New York City and the Pentagon on September 11, 2001. Through television, the images of war have been vividly imprinted on our minds. The words "forsaken" and "desolate" are well chosen.

In some ways, I believe the church today is in captivity…to the world and its system. A report released by Christian market researcher George Barna noted some discouraging results concerning the church in the United States:

- Only 15% of those who regularly attend a Christian church ranked their relationship with God as the top priority in their life.
- 3 out of every 4 teenagers have engaged in at least one type of psychic or witchcraft-related activity (Ouija board, reading books, playing sorcery/witchcraft games, palm reading). Interestingly, fewer than 3 of every 10 churched teenagers have received teaching from their church concerning the supernatural.
- A comparison of people's faith before and after 9/11 showed 5 years after the attack, there was statistically little change in faith-related areas such as religious behaviors, beliefs, spiritual commitment, and self-identity[8].

According to Barna's research, American Christians are not as dedicated to their faith as they like to believe. While they feel faith is important, "their faith is rarely the focal point of their life or a critical factor in their decision-making."[9]

I share these statistics only to point out that the enemy of our souls would like nothing better than to hold the church captive to the system he has deceptively set in place in the world.

Forsaken and Desolate

In Hebrew, the word, "forsaken" pictures a divorced or widowed woman of that culture and time. It speaks of a sense of bereavement, of being discarded, deserted, rejected, and alone. Isaiah 54:6: *For the Lord has called you like a woman forsaken and grieved in spirit, like a youthful wife when you were refused.*

Women who were divorced or widowed had no means of support and were often destitute. Forced to exist under a shroud of shame, they lived without love, without a sense of value, and without hope. "Desolate" is an equally harsh word. It speaks of devastation, barrenness, no life, and no future…a wasteland.

Both terms are names of reproach and shame. I couldn't help but think as I read of the condition of Jerusalem during the captivity, "Hasn't this been the identity of many in the church?" So many Christians have lived their lives from a place of reproach and shame.

Reproach is the opposite of favor. It means to find fault with, blame, criticize, disapprove of, discredit. It speaks to us of condemnation and judgmentalism, of living with regret and shame over the failures and mistakes of the past.

I believe one of the most effective tools the enemy uses to keep us ineffective for God is condemnation. If he can keep you bound by an identity that has been distorted by brokenness, rejection, abandonment, trauma, or loss, he can hinder you from coming into the fullness of the identity God had in mind when He engraved your design on the tapestry of your life.

If the enemy can keep you from your identity in God, he can also keep you from fully inheriting the destiny God has for you. The place God has purposed just for you in His ongoing plan in the earth will be left vacant.

Tangled Threads

The fabric of my identity was woven from a background of dysfunction, alcoholism, and domestic violence. All I could see was the underside of my tapestry with tangled threads, frayed ends, and stitches that seemed to go nowhere. I grew up without a sense of security because of the conflict in my parents' marriage. My father was physically in the home until I was 12 years old when they divorced, but he was not present emotionally or spiritually.

If the enemy can keep you from your identity in God, he can also keep you from fully inheriting the destiny God has for you.

It wasn't until years later that I realized the impact that had on my identity. I learned that a father's influence on his daughter has the greatest imprint on her identity as a woman. Because I lacked a healthy relationship with my father, I grew up with a rather unusual concept of myself. Whenever I pictured how I looked, my face was a blank oval with no distinguishing features. I did not feel I was recognizable.

Because of that, I would never approach someone I knew unless I was absolutely sure he knew who I was. It was too risky…being "faceless" meant others wouldn't recognize me and then I would feel foolish.

Remember the difference between head and heart knowledge? I knew intellectually my face had distinctive features, but my behavior of not speaking to someone reflected the belief in my heart. This was not a conscious awareness. I simply acted out of what was in my heart. This distorted self-concept of being less than, or of little value, was one I carried with me into adulthood. But as I will share in a later chapter, God is able to heal the most broken of His children and fully unravel all the tangled threads.

The Lie

The enemy weaves his intentions into our lives as well. He weaves his lie. I mentioned in the first chapter that most of us heard the lie before we heard the truth, so that now, we hear the truth of God through the lie. That means we filter the truth of the Bible through a belief system that has been affected by the lie of the enemy.

He uses the lie to keep you from discovering and embracing all God created you to be.

God has a purpose for your life, but so does Satan. His purpose is to distort, diminish, or destroy the image of God in you. If he can succeed, you will be one less person reflecting the light of Christ in the earth. Satan's strategy is to try to hinder God's plan and purpose from going forth in the earth…to keep the light of the gospel hidden.

What is the lie? It is a belief system that says:

1. You are not enough.
2. God is not enough to make you enough.
3. You need something from the world to make you enough.[10]

It began back in the Garden. The implication to Eve when tempted to partake of the fruit of the Tree of the Knowledge of Good and Evil was, "You are not enough the way you are. There is something lacking in you, you are not adequate or sufficient." The enemy also insinuated that God was not able to make her enough. The conclusion? She needed something from the world (the fruit) to make her sufficient. We have been believing the lie ever since.

The basis of the lie and its insidious intent is to cause us to live out of an identity of shame. Shame says there is something inherently wrong with me; I am flawed, damaged goods. The strong feeling attached to shame is that of being unlovable and worthless. It is different from guilt in that guilt focuses on the action (I made a mistake). Shame focuses on the person (I am a mistake).

Mephibosheth

There was a young man in the Bible who was well acquainted with shame. His name was Mephibosheth. His story is rich with insight for us today. When he was 5 years old, his grandfather, King Saul, and his father, Jonathan, were killed. The Word tells us that his nurse picked him up and they fled. But as she hurried to leave, she dropped him, and Mephibosheth fell and became lame in both feet (2 Samuel 4:4, NCV).

Interesting that it was a nurse – one who cares for the sick, brings comfort, healing, and a safe environment – who dropped him. God had created a "safe" environment for the highest of His creation. But just as Mephibosheth "fell" from his nurse, so man "fell" and has been "lame" ever since. Mephibosheth was 5 years old when he fell. Five is the number for grace. Even during the Fall, God had made provision for grace.

The story goes on to tell us Mephibosheth was taken in and cared for by a wealthy man who lived in Lo Debar. Lo Debar means "pastureless" and speaks of a barren land.

So, here was a boy born to royalty living by the mercy of a wealthy landowner, in a barren place. Mephibosheth was unable to care for even his basic necessities such as bathing and providing food for himself. He had to be carried wherever he went because he could not walk.

Labeled

In several scriptures that refer to him, it states, Mephibosheth, who was lame in his feet. It is as if his lameness was the identifying factor of his life. He was "labeled" – LAME.

Many of God's people today live with places of "lameness" that may not show on the outside. Their walk has been hindered by the wounds they've experienced in life. They live with labels from the past:

You know Barb, she's the one who's been divorced twice…

Jim, the one you can never depend on…

Mary, the one who was abused…

Even though they may have found grace to be healed, many find themselves living in a barren place, with the "lameness" and labels of the past defining who they are. Like Mephibosheth, they, too, were born to royalty. They need their King to come and recognize them for who they truly are, just as David did for Mephibosheth.

In his desire to honor his covenant with his friend, Jonathan, David called for any descendants that were still alive from the house of Saul. Mephibosheth was brought to him. Listen to the shame in Mephibosheth's heart as he approaches David: *What is your servant that you should look upon such a dead dog as I?* (2 Sam 9:8). The phrase "dead dog" signified a person of no value. But David looks beyond the lameness and sees the heritage of a king.

3 Promises

David makes 3 promises to Mephibosheth (2 Sam 9:1-13).

- **RESTORE:** *[I] will restore to you all the land of Saul your grandfather...* (2 Sam 9:7)

  David would give back to Mephibosheth all that was taken from him – his inheritance. So our King restores what the enemy has taken from us:

  Instead of their shame, my people will receive a double portion, And instead of disgrace, they will rejoice in their inheritance; And so they will inherit a double portion in their land, and everlasting joy will be theirs. (Isaiah 61:7 NIV)

- **SUSTAIN:** *...you shall eat bread at my table continually* (2 Sam 9:7).

  Mephibosheth would no longer lack sustenance. So our King provides all we need:

  And Jesus said to them, "I am the bread of life. He who comes to Me shall never hunger, and he who believes in Me shall never thirst. (John 6:35-36)

  The Lord is my shepherd; I shall not want. (Psalms 23:1)

- **REGAIN:** *...like one of the king's sons* (2 Samuel 9:11). Mephibosheth regains his true identity as a part of the king's family. So our King paid the price to redeem our true identity as part of God's royal family.

  Eph 1:5-7...*having predestined us to adoption as sons by Jesus Christ to Himself, according to the good pleasure of His will, 6 to the praise of the glory of His grace, by which He made us accepted in the Beloved. 7 In Him we have redemption through His blood...*

  Eph 3:14-16: *For this reason I bow my knees to the Father of our Lord Jesus Christ, 15 from whom the whole family in heaven and earth is named...*

The beautiful story of Mephibosheth, whose name means *"Dispeller of Shame,"* shows us David as a type of our King, Jesus, who comes to us in our lameness, our forsakenness (shame) and desolation (barrenness), in order to redeem, restore, and bring us to our Father's table so that we may enjoy the Bread of Life forever.

The strongest antidote for shame is a revelation of God's love for you personally. I'm convinced it was knowing and experiencing God's love firsthand that enabled David to give it freely to Mephibosheth. God's unconditional love made David a man after God's own heart.

Healed to Serve

In the Old Testament system of sacrifices, an animal who was lame was disqualified from being used as an offering (Lev. 22:20-23). Similarly, the descendents of Aaron who were lame were considered unfit for service (Lev. 21:16-21). As a nation of priests and kings (1 Peter 2:9, Rev. 1:6), we are to be living sacrifices (Rom. 12:1), and for that reason, it is crucial that we allow God to both reveal and then heal the places of lameness in our lives. His unconditional love and His acceptance will bring wholeness that we may serve Him and make Him known.

Matt 5:48 (The Message):

In a word, what I'm saying is, Grow up. You're kingdom subjects. Now live like it. Live out your God-created identity. Live generously and graciously toward others, the way God lives toward you.

Let's Talk About It

1. Can you relate to the terms, "forsaken" and "desolate?" In what ways?
2. How has the enemy used the lie to weave "tangled threads" into your life?
3. Identify specific areas where the enemy has caused you to feel "you are not enough."

 ## At Home This Week

1. Give the Holy Spirit permission to show you where you have been entangled in the lie. Then make a choice – a commitment in prayer – to no longer live in the lie, but to live in the power of the truth.
2. Meditate on Ephesians, chapter one. Ask the Holy Spirit to quicken to your heart those verses He wants to weave into the fabric of your being.

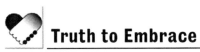 ## Truth to Embrace

1. The enemy of our souls would like nothing better than to hold the church captive to the system he has deceptively set in place in the world.
2. God is able to heal the most broken of His children and fully unravel all the tangled threads.

5

Discolored Threads

As I mentioned in the previous chapter, the enemy comes to distort and even destroy our identity. Using a variety of deceptions to communicate his lie, they become discolored threads in the tapestry of our life. Let me highlight a few.

Words

Proverbs 18:21 states, *Death and life are in the power of the tongue.* Often we fail to realize the power of our words. Parents, teachers, siblings, and peers say things that can affect our identity. Counselors' files are filled with stories of people who have had negative words spoken over their lives as youngsters, only to watch the fulfillment walked out in their adult lives. Words such as, "You'll never amount to anything," "Why can't you get good grades like your sister/ brother?" have the capacity to communicate a message that impacts the very identity of a child. Words become beliefs, and beliefs direct our lives.

> Death and life
> are in the
> power of
> the tongue.
> Proverbs 18:21

As the scripture says, words also have the power to impart life and blessing in a person's life. God's Word has the power to heal our misshapen self-perception and to impart truth about who we are.

Psalm 107:20...*He sent His word and healed them.*

Looks

Do you know that a look can express approval or disapproval and consequently impact our self-concept? Looks, or facial expressions, convey an attitude of the heart. Much of what we communicate is not so much in the words we say, but in other means of communication: body language, tone of voice, feelings, and attitudes.

When I was in third grade, I proudly came to school one day with a new pair of shoes that I thought were wonderful. At one point during the day, I had to go up to the teacher's desk. When I did, my teacher looked at me, then looked down at my shoes, then looked at me again and turned her head away. I was crushed. The look of disapproval on her face was such that I never did feel acceptable in that classroom for the rest of the school year.

Even a look can affect our identity.
Psalms 33:13-16
(13) The LORD looks from heaven;
He sees all the sons of men.
(14) From the place of His dwelling He looks on all the inhabitants
of the earth;
(15) He fashions their hearts individually;
He considers all their works.

The Word also tells us that the Lord guides us with His eye
(Psalm 32:8).

Touch

Touch can have an impact on our identity. There are loving, nurturing kinds of touch that communicate love, acceptance, warmth, security, and build trust. But there are also inappropriate kinds of touch that do untold damage to the identity of a child. Abuse distorts a person's self-concept at the very core of their being, which is why it is so destructive. It not only harms the physical body, it ravages the soul.

I once ministered to a woman who had been so devastated by abuse that she could not even say the words, "Jesus loves me" until we had prayed and ministered to her for several minutes.

Jesus longs to touch us by His Holy Spirit and heal the devastation in our lives.

Luke 6:19…*And the whole multitude sought to touch Him, for power went out from Him and healed them all.*

Neglect

Physical and emotional neglect, abandonment, lack of nurturing, all impact a person's identity. The absence of needed care, whether deliberate or unintentional, is just as damaging to the identity of a child as abuse. It can leave one with a sense of incompleteness, emptiness, and worthlessness that distorts the child's self-perception, just as a missed stitch in a tapestry mars the beauty of the work.

'The women had no faces… no identity. They were just anonymous figures in black."

These missing pieces lead the person into a lifetime of seeking to satisfy the empty places in unfulfilling ways.

God wants to fill those places left void through neglect and abandonment.

Psalms 27:10…*When my father and my mother forsake me, Then the LORD will take care of me.*

The word translated "care" in this verse is a Hebrew word meaning to cure, recover, put everything together.[11] It speaks of the Lord's restoration of the places of "lameness" in our lives.

Cultural Messages

There are nations in the world where a person's value depends upon gender. Little girls are of no consequence. As a result, they are not given even the basic necessities of food and clothing if it means a little boy will go without.

In his book, *Why Not Women?*, Loren Cunningham, founder of Youth With A Mission (YWAM), notes that "450 million women are physically impaired due to childhood malnutrition. In many societies, girls and their mothers eat only after the men and boys are fed."[12]

In Afghanistan, the now fallen Taliban government had forbidden, by law, the education of females and had prohibited women from working outside the home. Those without husbands to support them had no means of livelihood. Many committed suicide. Women were isolated from the world and literally became prisoners in their own homes, unable to venture outside. If they did, they had to be covered from head to foot in thick veils. Before the Taliban's rule, many of these women attended universities and were highly educated. Many held prestigious positions as doctors and lawyers.

Mr. Cunningham recounts an experience he had on an airplane as he flew into the capital of one of the most restrictive Middle Eastern nations. When the Swiss Air flight left Zurich, all the men and women were dressed in Western clothing.

As the plane neared its final destination, the women began disappearing into the restrooms to emerge covered from head to foot in "chadors" – thick, black veils.

Mr. Cunningham states:

"The women had no faces. They had no identity. They were just anonymous figures shrouded in black."[13]

There are cultures in which a woman is looked on as nothing more than a piece of property to be used at the discretion of the owner (her husband). There are religions that teach women that they are inferior to men intellectually, spiritually, and in every other way. The identity of millions of women throughout the world has been destroyed through the lie that the enemy has disseminated through their culture or religion.

Even in Western culture, we receive messages daily about what it means to be a woman. Standards are set through the media, magazines, radio and TV, movies, the fashion world. Case in point:

in the 1950s the epitome of female beauty was the full-figured Marilyn Monroe. Did you know Marilyn wore a size 14 dress?!

One decade later, a tall British model, aptly named Twiggy, set a whole new standard of female beauty. Her stick-like figure was a radical departure from the curvy, voluptuous figure of the 1950s. We've been living under that 60's image ever since!

Men, too, receive cultural messages that affect their identity. "Real men don't cry" or show emotion. Sports figures are held up as role models to emulate. What does that say to the boy who is not athletic? Think of all the cultural messages we receive every day that establish a standard for men and women that most can never live up to.

These are just a few of the deceptions through which the enemy seeks to exert negative influence on our identity. The result? We live out of a distorted or unclear image of who we are, instead of who God created us to be.

Rick Joyner, founder of MorningStar Ministries and recognized prophetic voice to the body of Christ, stated:

One reason for the explosive increase of lawlessness and suicide that we are seeing in the emerging generation is because they lack a clear identity and purpose. Because we were created for the Lord and to have fellowship with God who is Spirit, we can never find true peace or fulfillment until we are walking in our purpose in the Lord.[14]

The Master Weaver

God, in His infinite wisdom and unfailing love, pulls all the discolored and tangled threads the enemy and the world have sewn into our lives, and begins to weave His truth, His purpose, and His design into us. The enemy's plan to distort, destroy and diminish the image of God in us will never succeed as long as we open our hearts to the Holy Spirit and allow the unraveling to take place so that restoration can come. Proverbs 21:30 (NIV) assures us that, *There is no wisdom, no insight, no plan that can succeed against the LORD.*

Let's Talk About It

1. Can you identify the "discolored threads" the enemy has used to distort your identity? Share one or two experiences.
2. Are you ready to disentangle yourself from the lie and come into the power of the truth about who you are in Christ?
3. Pray one for another, committing yourself to the work of the "Master Weaver" as He unravels threads that were not of His choosing and weaves new ones in their place.

 ## At Home This Week

We have identified 5 specific ways in which the enemy communicates his lie to us. Interestingly, in their book, The Blessing[15] Gary Smalley and John Trent identify 5 parts of parental blessing intended to impart God's love and identity into a person's life. Meditate on each one, asking your heavenly Father to express His blessing to your heart.

1. Meaningful touch – warm and nurturing physical touch (God can touch our spirit and soul).
2. Spoken word – words of affirmation, blessing, love, acceptance, and encouragement (Through His Word and His people).
3. Expressing high value – acknowledging the intrinsic worth and value of the person (He can give understanding of our value in Him).
4. Picturing a special future – expressing hope for the future (His plan and destiny for our life).
5. An active commitment – a commitment to helping the person realize their full identity and destiny in the Lord. (His commitment to us is unending – Phil 1:6).

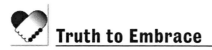 **Truth to Embrace**

1. Much of what we communicate is not so much in the words we say, but in other means of communication: body language, tone of voice, feelings, and attitude.

2. There are nations in the world where a person's value depends upon gender. Little girls are of no consequence.

3. There is no wisdom, no insight, no plan that can succeed against the Lord (Proverbs 21:30).

6

Worldly Designs

I mentioned in Chapter One that within each one of us is a deep need for security and significance. These two elements shape our identity and can be fulfilled only in God.

Often, life's painful experiences make it difficult to believe that God would love us unconditionally and that He has a design and purpose for our life. Longing to fill the void inside, we embrace the third part of the lie (you need something from the world to make you enough) and go looking for love, value, and acceptance in all the wrong places. We turn to the world to satisfy our need and define who we are. 1 John 2:15

Do not love the world or the things in the world. If anyone loves the world, the love of the Father is not in him.

> ...loving the world... means accepting the world's system of determining our value.

We typically think of this scripture in terms of material things or overt acts of sin. However, loving the world also means accepting the world's system of determining our value. The enemy has constructed the world's system in such a way that it will always leave us feeling like we don't measure up in one or many ways. Let me share a few of the places the enemy leads us to believe we will find identity and value.

Accomplishments

In Luke 10, we read the account of Jesus sending 70 of his

disciples on a short-term mission trip. He gave explicit instructions on what luggage to take (none!) (v. 4), how to greet potential recipients of their ministry (v. 5), how to handle honorariums (v. 7-8), and exactly how to minister (v. 9). He even told them how to deal with rejection (v. 10-12). It seems it was a successful mission trip because the seventy returned excited over the fact that the demons were subject to them, in Jesus' name (v. 17).

What a sense of power must have come from accomplishing such ministerial exploits! Jesus' response? He reminded them that the real cause for rejoicing was that their names were written in the Book of Life – more important than what they did was who they were!

How easy it is for us to define ourselves by the things we have accomplished. There is a fine line between the sense of satisfaction that comes from knowing you are following God's will and have done your best, and striving for accomplishment in order to feel accepted and valued.

One of the ways you can sometimes distinguish between the two is to ask yourself this question: How important is it that others know what I've accomplished? It's not wrong to take joy in a job well done, as long as it is not the source of your identity.

Who we are in Him

Mike Bickle, pastor and founder of the House of Prayer, in Kansas City, MO, stated that God wants us to be relationally oriented first and achievement oriented second. Yes, we are to fulfill the Great Commission, but who we are *in* Him is far more important than what we do *for* Him. In fact, who we are will dramatically impact what we do.[16]

Performance

In his book, *The Search for Significance,* Robert McGee formulates the world's equation for finding identity: Self Worth = Performance + Others' Opinions.[17] How well we perform and please others determines how we feel about ourselves. This is a trap that causes us to struggle continually to live up to a certain standard.

On one end of the performance spectrum is the person who strives for perfectionism: everything must be done with perfection, without flaw. Driven from the inside to achieve success on the outside, often there is a fear of failing. Failure causes feelings of worthlessness and unacceptability. Nothing less than perfect will do.

We listen to the negative voices that urge us to prove our worth by doing something relevant, spectacular, powerful. To experience the love and respect you crave, you have to earn it! Second-best will never do. Drivenness. That strategy may seem to work for a time, but the result is ultimately unfulfilling and doesn't satisfy.

Success is not final, failure is not fatal: it is the courage to continue that counts (Winston Churchill).

> God does not respond to our performance, He responds to our heart.

Wrong Belief

Because of this wrong belief that our identity is dependent upon how well we perform, we even approach our relationship with God from a performance base.

Have you ever felt distanced from God because you were not spending enough time reading the Bible, or praying? Have you ever felt God was mad at you because you failed to resist a temptation? God does not respond to our performance, He responds to our heart.

No Clipboard

God doesn't have a giant clipboard with a checklist of chores He expects us to perform before we can enter His presence. He invites us into His presence freely with open arms, eager to be with us.

Several years ago when my grandson was about two years old, I was driving home from work one night thinking about seeing him when I arrived. Anyone who's been around two-year-olds knows they are not perfect! My grandson was no exception. Yet, as I drove home, it seemed the traffic lights took longer than usual that night, the cars in front of me moved slower…I was so anxious to see him. I pictured walking in the door and him running to me, arms reaching out, waiting to be picked up. I smiled at the thought. My heart was warmed.

In that moment, the Lord spoke to my heart saying, "The way you feel about Zach is just how I feel about you. I can't wait to be with you and spend time together." I've learned something else about time with my Father…it doesn't have to be long, protracted periods of time, although those are good, too. Even a few moments, giving Him my full attention, telling Him I love Him, delights His heart and mine.

A two-year-old won't stay in your arms for very long before he's wiggling to run and play, but, oh, those few moments of holding him close! What joy it brought to my heart. That's how your Father feels about you!

Position or Title

Deriving a sense of value because of a position we hold, whether in business or ministry, or a title we have, is looking for identity in the wrong places.

Many have relied so heavily on their position or title that if it is taken away, they feel they have no value. The business world applauds this mindset, encouraging young people to "climb the corporate ladder." Unfortunately, many reach the top only to find it doesn't meet the need they thought it would. It turns out to be one of those threads that seem to go nowhere!

Desire to be Above Others

Even two of Jesus' closest disciples, James and John, experienced this need. Although they were part of His inner circle, they longed to have a special position with Him for all eternity because they asked, ...*Grant us that we may sit, one on Your right and the other on Your left, in Your glory* (Mark 10:37).

Needing to have a distinguished title or position is wanting to be above others, and rather than fostering unity, it can create relational problems. Read the account of this incident to see how the other 10 disciples reacted to James' and John's request. They were not pleased!

Along a similar line is feeling a sense of value or importance by knowing someone in a highly visible position or a position of authority. Being close to those "at the top" lends a false sense of significance. You can see this need in someone if they are in the habit of "name dropping."

Psalms 4:3 states, *But know that the LORD has set apart for Himself* [emphasis added] *him who is godly.* He has not set us apart for a job, a position, or even a ministry. He has first of all set us apart for Himself, for intimate relationship with Him.

Education, Intelligence

Some define themselves by the letters that follow their name, such as Ph.D., or the number of degrees they hold. While I strongly believe that education is vital in the development of a person and can help lead to a fulfilling life, I also believe it is not the sole determinant of what someone has to offer.

Role Model

Henri Nouwen, who was one of the great spiritual writers of our day, is a beautiful example of a person who possessed all the accolades academia had to offer, yet found the true meaning and value of life in a community of mentally handicapped adults who had no understanding of his academic accomplishments. Nor were they impressed by them.

He authored over 25 books, taught at the University of Notre Dame, Yale, and Harvard, and lectured around the world. Yet, through the last several years of his life serving as pastor in a community of mentally disabled people, he learned that the ones he had gone to help were the very ones who taught him the most.

1 Corinthians 8:1.

Knowledge puffs up, but love edifies.

Gifts or Talents

Do you ever find a sense of value in being known as a prophet, skilled intercessor, leader, or a teacher? As we'll see in Chapter 9, it is important to know our gifting and use those God-given gifts and abilities to advance His kingdom, but we cannot derive our identity from our gifts.

Unless we know who we are in Him and have allowed Him to develop His name and His character in us, even His gifts can become a snare to us (see 1 Corinthians 13:1-10). It has been said that character is God's inoculation against His awesome power flowing through mere human beings.

There are many other things we could list from which we try to find acceptance and value, such as physical appearance, money, possessions, fame, or recognition, but one of the avenues we seek identity most is through other people.

People

Every person in our life has the potential of weaving a thread into the tapestry of who we are, a thread that distorts or a thread that enhances.

Parents

Beginning with our family, the words of parents, as well as their hopes and dreams for our lives, affect our identity.

Relationships are the fabric of our life. We feel like a whole person when all the pieces are in their proper place. Sometimes there are small rips in the family fabric but they're patched or sewn up and you go on.

But when a significant member of the family isn't there, or isn't who they should be, the entire fabric of the family is torn, often from top to bottom. Mother and Father are significant members. The empty place in our life can be carried for years.[18]

Have you ever known someone who pursued a particular career, such as a doctor, lawyer, politician, because it was the desire of his/her parent(s)? Some children grow up with expectations that they will continue the family business, or be in ministry like their parents, grandparents, and even great-grandparents before them. Until a few short decades ago, most little girls grew up believing that their only identity as adults would be that of a wife and mother.

Parental influence can be either a positive or negative force in helping to shape our identity. The negative impact would be to reach adulthood only to find the plans and goals were those of the parents. The positive side would be the parents' encouragement of the potential gift they recognize in their child. Providing opportunities for development through training and special classes would strengthen and affirm the child's unique identity.

> ....character is God's inoculation against His awesome power flowing though mere human beings.

Others

There are others in our lives whose influence can impact our identity: spouses, relatives, teachers, siblings, peers, employers, etc. In their struggle for independence, teens will often reject their parents' opinion but conform to the standard set by their peers. As adults, we may so admire someone that we try to be like them, or strive for their approval.

A note in the *Life Recovery Bible* states it clearly: *Many of us have spent our lives trying to be someone we are not... Maybe we have difficulty accepting our personality, our appearance, our handicaps,* even our talents. *Perhaps we spend our energy and time trying to be what someone else wants us to be because we feel that who we are is not enough.*[19]

Whenever we attempt to find our value in what another person thinks of us, we are really looking to that person to give us a sense of respect and dignity.

Clothed With Beauty

(He) redeems your life from the pit and corruption; (He) beautifies, dignifies, and crowns you with loving-kindness and tender mercies (Psalm 103:4 Amplified).

Dignity is the quality of being worthy of esteem or honor. It means stateliness, proper pride and self-respect.[20] We need to understand that the dignity we long for never will be found in the esteem of other people. Only through knowing who we are in Him, and more importantly, who He is in us, will we find our true worth. In looking to people, we sabotage the very way to true dignity, esteem, honor, and self-respect.

Psalm 103:4 pictures God clothing us with beauty and dignity. When we look to people to clothe us with those qualities, the best they can do is cover us with a brash, garish beauty, like a costume or clothing fad that quickly loses its attraction. And like a fashion fad that comes and goes and leaves you shopping for the next new item, you'll find you must keep getting more and more affirmation from people to make you feel good about yourself. It is one of the ways we give our identity over to others and look to them to define us. But God will clothe us with beauty and dignity from within. It is not an outward dignity, but an inward, eternal quality that will never fade or go out of style.

1 Peter 3:3-5

Do not let your adornment be merely outward—arranging the hair, wearing gold, or putting on fine apparel—rather let it be the hidden person of the heart, with the incorruptible beauty of a gentle and quiet spirit, which is very precious in the sight of God.

I like the way one author describes the challenge before us:
You are questing for wholeness and a healthy autonomy from the expectations of others.[21]

Let's Talk About It

1.   Have you pursued any of the "worldly designs" mentioned in this chapter? Which ones?
2.   Are there certain people in your life, such as authority figures (parents, teachers, employers, etc.), whose acceptance and approval are necessary for you to feel good about yourself? Name them and explain why their opinion is so important to you.
3.   The world's equation for finding identity is: Self Worth = Performance + Others' Opinions. Based on the truth of God's Word, formulate a new equation for your identity.

 At Home This Week

Focus your prayer this week on asking God to show you the ways you pursue "worldly designs" or ways you look to the world to make you feel you are valuable and worthwhile.

Expect the Holy Spirit to quicken this to your mind in situations you encounter throughout the week.

Purpose to respond to each circumstance based on God's truth about your identity, not the enemy's or the world's.

 Truth to Embrace

1. Whenever we attempt to find our value in what another person thinks of us, we are really looking to him or her to give us a sense of respect and dignity.
2. God doesn't have a giant clipboard with a checklist of chores He expects us to accomplish before we can enter His presence.
3. The Lord tells us that who we are in Him is far more important than what we do for Him.

7

Broken Threads

Looking for love in all the wrong places results in broken threads. When we live our lives from a distorted or unclear identity and subsequently look for something from the world to make us feel worthwhile, acceptable or "enough," one of the effects can be behavior that results in relational problems. If we really knew in our hearts who we are in God – that is, experienced His unconditional, unfailing love for us personally, and knew His plan and purpose for our life – some of the issues I will touch on would be minimized, or perhaps even non-existent. Let me share a few with you.

Comparison

Not being at peace with who we are in God leads us to compare ourselves continually with one another. If we try to compare ourselves to other parts of God's tapestry, or if we try to make ourselves look like the other "stitches," we deprive God and the world of the color, texture, and design that is in us. Relationally, when we compare, we put people on different "levels" and interact with them accordingly.

> Comparing often leads to competing.

People you deem to be above you may cause you to relate to them with a feeling of inferiority or perhaps even intimidation. Others may be on a lower level, they've not come as far as you, or do not have the knowledge or experience you have. Consequently, you may feel superior to them. In that case, you might not be as

•71•

open to hearing what they have to offer or share.

Comparing doesn't allow you to relate to others on a person-to-person, heart-to-heart basis, so the relationship is less than genuine. It can also keep you from using your gifts as effectively as you might. Silenced by intimidation, the portion you have to bring remains hidden. The Word says it is not wise to compare ourselves one to another (2 Corinthians 10:12).

Competition

Comparing can lead to competing. You feel a need to prove yourself, to show that you are just as capable as the one with whom you're comparing yourself. You want to present yourself in such a way as to impress. While competition in athletic endeavors may produce champions, in the context of Christian relationship it is deadly. Instead of working together, we work against each other in order to come out on top. We can't have open, trusting relationships with those whom we're competing against. Strife and division are the result.

Mark 9:33-35

(33) Then He came to Capernaum. And when He was in the house He asked them, "What was it you disputed among yourselves on the road?" (34) But they kept silent, for on the road they had disputed among themselves who would be the greatest. (35) And He sat down, called the twelve, and said to them, "If anyone desires to be first, he shall be last of all and servant of all."

Self Promotion

If you feel you lack the recognition you deserve, you may tend to promote yourself in order to receive the affirmation you are seeking. You want people to know how successful (or gifted or intelligent or talented) you are so that you can feel good about yourself.

James 3:13-18

(13) Who is wise and understanding among you? Let him show by

good conduct that his works are done in the meekness of wisdom. (14)
But if you have bitter envy and selfish ambition in your hearts, do not
boast and lie against the truth. (15) This wisdom does not descend from
above, but is earthly, sensual, demonic. (16) For where envy and self-
seeking exist, confusion and every evil thing are there. (17) But the
wisdom that is from above is first pure, then peaceable, gentle, willing
to yield, full of mercy and good fruits, without partiality and without
hypocrisy. (18) Now the fruit of righteousness is sown in peace by those
who make peace.

Covetousness

Living with a self-perception that is distorted by shame and reproach can breed the sin of covetousness. Covetousness, simply put,
is longing to be in someone else's situation or to have what they
have. It can be jealousy over a friend's happy marriage and longing
to have that, or envying the material success of another.

In ministry, it can mean wanting the anointing or gifts of a
brother or sister. In essence, it is being discontent with what you
have or who you are.

Hebrews 13:5

(5) Let your conduct be without covetousness; be content with such
things as you have. For He Himself has said, "I will never leave you nor
forsake you."

Luke 12:15

(15) And He said to them, "Take heed and beware of covetousness,
for one's life does not consist in the abundance of the things he possesses."

Judging

Jesus said, *Judge not, that you be not judged; For with what judg-*
ment you judge, you will be judged; (Matthew 7:1-2).

The word, "judge," means to condemn, criticize, or punish. One
of the primary reasons we judge is because we do not feel the security of unconditional love.

Henri Nouwen expresses it beautifully:

Can we free ourselves from the need to judge others? Yes…by claiming for ourselves the truth that we are the beloved daughters and sons of God.

As long as we continue to live as if we are what we do, what we have, and what other people think about us, we will remain filled with judgments, opinions, evaluations, and condemnations. We will remain addicted to the need to put people and things in their "right" place.

To the degree that we embrace the truth that our identity is not rooted in our success, power, or popularity, but in God's infinite love, to that degree can we let go of our need to judge.[22]

Concluding Truth

What can we conclude from this chapter? That the lie of the enemy that drives us to seek our identity in the things the world has to offer will never satisfy the deep longing in our hearts. By its very design it will leave us empty and continually running after more success, more affirmation, more recognition.

> …those earthly sources become idols in our lives…

This reminds me of the "black holes" scientists have discovered in space. A black hole is a region of space in which the gravitational pull is the so powerful that nothing, not even light, can escape. They are like bottomless chasms that can never be filled. Our hearts can be like those "black holes"…try as we might, we can never fill them with earthly sources of fulfillment.

In actuality, those earthly sources become idols in our lives, occupying the place in our hearts designed to be held by the One who made us. Only God's limitless love can satisfy our need for security. Only God's purpose for us can give meaning and significance to our life.

Ephesians 1:11

It's in Christ that we find out who we are and what we're living for. Long before we first heard of Christ and got our hopes up, he had his eye on us, had designs on us for glorious living, part of the overall purpose he is working out in everything and everyone (The Message).

A strong self-concept founded in God's love results in peace in our hearts, fulfillment in our lives, and healthy relationships as well. It provides a secure base from which to deepen your intimacy with God and relate to others in honesty, transparency, and vulnerability.

When you are confident in who you are in Him, then you are free to take responsibility for your own beliefs, emotions, attitudes and behavior without fear or condemnation. You can also allow others to be responsible for theirs without feeling guilty or responsible for how they feel. Healthy boundaries can be established that will diminish the need for damaging relational behavior such as manipulation and control.

You are free to relate to others as co-laborers, joint heirs, peers, instead of on different levels. You are free to take the place God has designed just for you in His body without worrying about what others are called to do.

Do you remember when Peter asked Jesus about John's future (John 21:22)? Jesus replied, *If I will that he remain till I come, what is that to you? You follow Me. In other words, embrace what I've called YOU to, and live in obedience to Me.*

Let's Talk About it

1. What relational behaviors can you relate to as "broken threads" in your life?
2. What relational damage has resulted from these wrong choices?
3. Describe how you might relate to someone if you knew with absolute certainty that you were completely accepted and deeply loved. Do you have such a relationship in your life with another person? With God?

 At Home This Week

Read through the book of Proverbs, listing verses that identify where your true security and significance are found.

 Truth to Embrace

1. Comparing doesn't allow you to relate to others on a person-to-person, heart-to-heart basis, so the relationship is less than genuine.
2. By its very design, the lie of the enemy will leave us empty and continually running after more success.
3. A strong self-concept founded in God's love results in peace in our hearts, fulfillment in our lives, and healthy relationships as well.

8

Threads of Purpose

When God fashioned us, He placed within each one special abilities, gifts and talents, natural and spiritual, that He desires to use for His glory. Our heavenly Father, from Whom comes every good gift and every perfect gift (James 1:17), has given us spiritual gifts that are meant to help us know and then fulfill, our part in His overall plan and purpose in the earth. Because no one else is created quite like you, with the unique blend of personality, gifts, talents, and abilities, there is no one else on earth that can fulfill your place in God's plan. So it is very important that you know the gifts He has placed within you, because they will be strong clues to your destiny in God. Let's take a brief look at spiritual gifts in the Bible.

> Because no one else is created quite like you...there is no one else on earth that can fulfill your place in God's plan.

Now concerning spiritual gifts, brethren, I do not want you to be ignorant: (1 Cor 12:1)

The Amplified Bible says it this way:

Now about the spiritual gifts (the special endowments of supernatural energy), brethren, I do not want you to be misinformed.

Not only are we to be knowledgeable about the spiritual gifts God has given us, but we are to pursue them:

But earnestly desire the best gifts (1 Cor 12:31).

"Earnestly desire" actually means to covet earnestly, to pursue, to strive after.[23] So we are to take this subject of spiritual gifts seriously, and we are to seek God for them.

First of all, **DISCOVER** what your gifts are (Rom. 12:1-3, Matt. 7:7-8, James 1:5), if you are not already aware of them. Secondly, be willing to **DEVELOP** your gifts (1 Tim.4:14a, 2 Tim 1:6). Thirdly, **DEPLOY**, or exercise your gifts (1 Pet.4:10, 1 Tim. 4:7b, Matt 25:14-30), for the strengthening of the body of Christ. Understanding how you are gifted also helps you to better understand others who have different gifts and whose ministry may look very different from yours.

Three Categories of Gifts

There are three listings of gifts in the Bible.

Motivational Gifts – Romans 12:4-8

Ministry Gifts – Ephesians 4:7-13

Manifestation Gifts – 1 Corinthians 12:8-11

Within the three categories of spiritual gifts listed in the Bible, we find:

The gifts of the Father – MOTIVATIONAL GIFTS – foundational, creation gifts, inherent in the believer. Romans 12:4-8: prophecy, serving, teaching, exhortation, giving, administration, mercy.

The gifts of the Son – OFFICE or MINISTRY GIFTS – given for the equipping of the saints and the ongoing work of the ministry. Ephesians 4:7-13: apostle, prophet, evangelist, pastor, teacher.

The gifts of the Holy Spirit – MANIFESTATION GIFTS – available and operative for all believers for the building up and edification of the church. 1 Corinthians 12:8-11: wisdom, knowledge, discerning of spirits, faith, healing, miracles, prophecy, tongues, interpretation of tongues.

All of these gifts, while diverse, are given by one Spirit. They come from the greatest gift – the Holy Spirit – and are visible evidence of His presence and activity in a believer's life.

In Paul's discussion of the Motivational Gifts, LOVE is emphasized (Rom. 12:9,10,18,21).

In Paul's discussion of the Office Gifts, LOVE is emphasized (Eph. 4:2,3,15,16).

In Paul's discussion of the Gifts of the Holy Spirit, LOVE is emphasized (1 Cor 13).

The point is that LOVE is the basis from which all gifts are to be exercised!

Because we are created in His image, every person has a spiritual gift, or more accurately, a mix of spiritual gifts. No one has all the gifts, but rather a combination of several, with one or two being dominant. The Bible likens the body of Christ to a physical body in Romans 12:5-6 and 1 Corinthians 12:12-30. The significance of this image is that it shows us that we need each other. Your gifts make up for the ones I lack and my gifts do the same for you. God intends us to be interdependent with each other – not dependent nor independent, but interdependent.

In this chapter, we will deal more fully with the Motivational Gifts because they relate more to our identity and who we are. They "move" us because they are part of our spiritual DNA. The Office Gifts and Manifestation Gifts relate more to our function in the body of Christ, or what we do, so we will just give a brief overview. For more information on these two categories of gifts, see the resources listed at the end of this book.

> ...every person has... a mix of spiritual gifts. No one has all the gifts, but rather a combination of several, with one or two being dominant.

Motivational Gifts

What do we mean by "Motivational Gifts"? These are spiritual gifts that motivate, or inspire or cause us to respond to life in a certain way. They are part of the way God "wired" us when He created us. For that reason, a teacher will approach a situation differently than someone gifted in mercy. As we look at each gift and the characteristics, strengths and weaknesses of each, hopefully you will be able to identity which gifts are part of the way God made you.

Prophecy/Perceiver

More aptly call the gift of perceiving, it has also been called the "insight" gift.

The Greek word, propheteia, means "the speaking forth of the mind and counsel of God."[24] As a motivational gift, it is the special ability given by the Father that enables a person to view life and circumstances with spiritual insight given by God.

— The motivation of the "perceiver" is:
  * to clearly perceive the will and counsel of God, to seek out the truth
  * uncover hindrances to spiritual growth so people can get right with God

  The Perceiver believes growth occurs by becoming aware of the sin in the heart, then repenting. They focus on spiritual principles and the fulfillment of God's plan.

— The need met in the body of Christ: SPIRITUAL

Characteristics (Strengths)
* Able to see past the outward to the inner motives of the heart
* Focus is on the eternal rather than temporal
* Tends to be strong, opinionated, black and white, strong sense of right and wrong
* Strict personal standards, lives life in a godly manner

Potential Pitfalls (Weaknesses)
* Focusing on the negative instead of the positive
* Can be judgmental and critical, especially of self
* Painfully blunt

— Examples of Perceivers in Scripture:
Anna (Luke 2:36-38),
John the Baptist (Luke 3:1-22, Matt 3:1-17)

— Favorite scripture of the Perceiver: Proverbs 28:13
A man who refuses to admit his mistakes can never be successful. But if he confesses and forsakes them, he gets another chance. (The Living Bible)

Serving/Ministry

This gift is the special ability God gives to minister to the needs of others.
The Greek word, diakonian, means "ministering."[25]

— The motivation of the "server" is to:
- Demonstrate love by meeting practical needs (i.e., food, shelter, comfort)
- Lend practical assistance to those in need

— The need met in the body: PRACTICAL

Characteristics (Strengths)
- Genuine love for others is expressed in deeds and actions
- Gives of self, time, and assets in order to meet the need
- Quick to identify and anticipate needs and then faithful and diligent to meet them
- Tends to be supportive of leadership

Potential Pitfalls (Weaknesses)
- Can be overcommitted, unable to say "no" to the neglect of own family
- Easily hurt or resentful when not appreciated
- Critical of others who don't see and meet obvious needs

— Examples of Servers in Scripture:
Martha (Luke 10:38-42, John 11:1-40, 12:2),
Stephen (Acts 6:1-4)

— Favorite scripture of the Server: Matt 25:35-40

35 For I was hungry, and you fed me. I was thirsty, and you gave me a drink. I was a stranger, and you invited me into your home. 36 I was naked, and you gave me clothing. I was sick, and you cared for me. I was in prison, and you visited me.'

37 "Then these righteous ones will reply, 'Lord, when did we ever see you hungry and feed you? Or thirsty and give you something to drink? 38 Or a stranger and show you hospitality? Or naked and give you clothing? 39 When did we ever see you sick or in prison and visit you?'

40 "And the King will say, 'I tell you the truth, when you did it to one of the least of these my brothers and sisters, you were doing it to me!'

(New Living Translation)

Teaching

This gift is the special ability God gives to be able to communicate truth in a way that is easy to understand and apply. The Greek word, didasko, means "to teach"[26] or "to give instruction."[27]

— The motivation of the "teacher" is to:
*   Search out and validate truth and impart that knowledge to others
*   Motivate others to consistently and enthusiastically study the Bible and assimilate its Truth

— The need met in the body is: MENTAL

Characteristics (Strengths)
*   Loves to learn, enjoys Bible study and research, validates truth from the Word
*   Presents truth in a way that is easily understood and applied, using illustrations from the Bible and presenting a comprehensive picture of the topic
*   Uneasy with subjective truth – begins with scripture and relates it to personal experience
*   Very conscientious about teaching the truth and not being in error

Potential Pitfalls (Weaknesses)
- "Knowledge puffs up" – can take credit for intelligence and knowledge gained through study
- Can be argumentative in an effort to know all the facts or because they don't accept another's teaching – critical of other teachers
- Need to verify every statement by scripture, hindering wider applications of the Word

— Examples of Teachers in Scripture:
Mary (Luke 10:39, John 11:45),
Apollos (Acts 18:24-28, 1 Cor 3:6)

— Favorite scripture of the Teacher: 2 Tim 2:15
Study and be eager and do your utmost to present yourself to God approved (tested by trial), a workman who has no cause to be ashamed, correctly analyzing and accurately dividing [rightly handling and skillfully teaching] the Word of Truth. (AMP)

Exhortation
This gift is "the special ability God gives to certain members of the Body of Christ to minister words of comfort, consolation, encouragement, and counsel to other members of the Body of Christ in such a way that they feel helped and healed."[28]
The Greek word, parakaleo, means "to come alongside of"[29] or "a calling to one's own side." It is the same Greek root from which we get the word, Parakletos: a term referring to the Holy Spirit, who comes alongside of us as Comforter and Counselor.

— The motivation of the "exhorter" is to:
- Encourage individuals to grow and mature spiritually
- Focus on meeting the personal psychological needs of the body through edifying, encouraging, and challenging
- Keep us aware of the importance of applying spiritual truth to our daily walk

— The need met in the body: PERSONAL

Characteristics (Strengths)
*   Enjoys counseling and encouraging people to grow, whether one-on-one, or through teaching or speaking
*   Gains insight through experience and validates it with Scripture
*   Accepts others where they are, non-judgmental
*   See trials and conflict as positive – an opportunity for growth

Potential Pitfalls (Weaknesses)
*   Can become frustrated or impatient when people don't change
*   Use scriptures out of context in order to make a point
*   Can be too outspoken, independent, or overly self-confident

— Examples of Exhorters in Scripture:
  Deborah (Judges 4, 5),
  Barnabas (Acts 4:36; 11:23-26)

— Favorite scripture of the Exhorter: Proverbs 25:11-12
  11 Timely advice is lovely,
  like golden apples in a silver basket.
  12 To one who listens, valid criticism
  is like a gold earring or other gold jewelry.
  (New Living Translation)

Giving

This gift is the special ability to contribute materially, above tithes and offerings, to the building of the Kingdom. It is not the kind of giving, such as tithes and offerings, that is expected of all Christians. It is the ability to give joyfully and generously to supply material needs.

The Greek word, metadidoomi, means "sharing of material possessions."[30]

— The motivation of the "giver" is to:
  *   Give to the physical needs of the body

- Contribute to others in order to support them in the extension of the Kingdom
- Entrust their own personal assets to others for the furtherance of the ministry

— The need met in the body: MATERIAL

Characteristics (Strengths)
- Generously gives money, possessions, time, and self to others by the leading of the Holy Spirit
- Sees God as their provider and source
- Prefers to give anonymously, without recognition
- Handles own finances and resources well

Potential Pitfalls (Weaknesses)
- May give away resources that are needed by the family
- Want to control the gift – wanting it to be used their way
- Can use giving to avoid other spiritual responsibilities

— Examples of the Givers in Scripture:
The widow who gave 2 mites (Mark 12:41-44),
Abraham (Genesis 13, 14, 22, 23, 24)

— Favorite scripture of the Giver: Proverbs 31:20
She extends her hand to the poor,
Yes, she reaches out her hands to the needy. (NKJV)

Administrator/Leader
This gift is the special ability God gives which enables the person to see the goals of a body and provide effective plans to accomplish those goals.
The Greek word, proistemi, literally means "to stand before" hence, "to lead, attend to" (indicating care and diligence), is translated "to rule" in Romans 12:8. It is also translated "maintain" in some instances (1 Timothy 3:8, 14).[31]

— The motivation of the "administrator" is to:
- Direct, or provide leadership, in the accomplishment of goals for the smooth and orderly operation of the church
- Coordinate the activities of others for the achievement of common goals
- Care for the functional tasks, organize people and resources in order to accomplish the goals and vision

– The need met in the body: Effectiveness, Leadership

Characteristics (Strengths)

> ...when you discover the gifts God has placed within you, you can then begin to develop them and exercise them for His glory.

- Highly motivated, organized, enthusiastic, efficient, and productive
- Focuses on the accomplishment of goals and gets the job done
- Take-charge type of person, has strong convictions, decisive, persuasive
- Able to see down the road, can visualize the resources and people necessary to accomplish the goal

Potential Pitfalls (Weaknesses)
- Can be too focused on goals and become insensitive to the needs of the workers
- "Workaholic" tendency – self-driven to the neglect of personal/family needs
- Micromanaging delegated tasks

— Examples of Administrators in Scripture:
The Proverbs Woman (Proverbs 31:10-31),
Nehemiah

— Favorite scripture of the Administrator:
1 Corinthians 14:40
Let all things be done decently and in order. (NKJV)

Mercy/Compassion

This gift is the special ability God gives "to feel genuine empathy and compassion for individuals, both Christian and non-Christian, who suffer distressing physical, mental or emotional problems, and to translate that compassion into cheerfully doing deeds that reflect Christ's love and alleviate suffering."[32]

The Greek word, eleeo, means "to feel sympathy with the misery of another," and especially sympathy manifested in act, or "to have pity or mercy on, to show mercy."[33]

— The motivation of the "mercy" gifted person is to:
  - Identify with and bring comfort and relief to those who are hurting or in distress.

— The need met in the body: EMOTIONAL

Characteristics (Strengths)
- Deep, feeling people, are ruled by the heart rather than the head
- Tender-hearted, focuses on the emotional and mental needs of those who are hurting
- Very accepting, looks for the good in others
- Rejoices in the blessings of others, grieves the pain of others

Potential Pitfalls (Weaknesses)
- Easily hurt by other's comments or attitudes
- Tendency to take up other people's offenses
- May rush in to relieve suffering and in so doing, hinder God's work in the person (human compassion vs. godly compassion)

— Examples in Scripture of those gifted in Mercy: Esther, The Good Samaritan (Luke 10:29-37)

— Favorite scripture of the Mercy person: Rom 12:15

Rejoice with those who rejoice [sharing others' joy], and weep with those who weep [sharing others' grief]. (AMP)

As we grow and mature, we may operate in any of the gifts at specific times. We may not all have the gift of exhortation, but we can certainly encourage one another. We may not all have the gift of serving, but we can all serve the body. We may not all have the gift of giving, but we should all give into the Kingdom. However, when you discover the gifts God has placed within you, you can then begin to develop them and exercise them for His glory.

Next is a very brief overview of the other two categories of gifts listed in the Word. As previously mentioned, for further teaching on these gifts, see the resources listed at the end of this book.

Office or Ministry Gifts

Ephesians 4:7-16

These gifts are referred to as the gifts of the Son because verse 8 states: *[Jesus] led captivity captive, And gave gifts to men.*

The word "gift" in Ephesians 4:8 is the Greek word doma and it means a present or a gift.[34] This word specifically refers to the Ministry, or Office Gifts, and refers to a person who is an equipper of the body of Christ. In other words, the "gift" is the person. These specially-endowed human "gifts" to the body of Christ are those whom God has called to lead and serve in the office of apostle, prophet, evangelist, pastor, and teacher. These leaders have the responsibility of equipping the saints (Eph. 4:12) and are important in seeing that the other 2 categories of gifts, listed in Romans 12:6-8 and 1 Corinthians 12:4-10, are applied in the body of Christ.

EQUIPPING means "making fit, preparing, training, perfecting, making fully qualified for service."[35] It has the sense in the original language of setting a bone during surgery. So equipping implies a recovered wholeness as when a broken limb is set and mends. The Great Physician is about making adjustments to His body so it will not be "out of joint." Part of the equipping work of these gifts is to help believers identify their personal gifting and understand how that fits with others, so that the body is joined and knit together by what every joint supplies, according to the effective working by which every part does its share, causes growth of the body for the edifying of itself in love (Eph 4:16).

> Love for God and His Body must be the motivating force behind using the gifts and abilities He has given us.

These Office Gifts are also referred to as the 5-fold ministry gifts. They are equipping ministries and are meant to work together, as a team, for the ultimate purpose of the church, as stated in Eph 4:13: *...till we all come to the unity of the faith and of the knowledge of the Son of God, to a perfect man, to the measure of the stature of the fullness of Christ.*

While any believer may, at times, be used to teach, prophesy, lead people to the Lord, or "pastor" others in the sense of caring for them, it does not mean he or she is called to the office of teacher, prophet, etc. Those who are called to serve in the capacity of an Office Gift have been commissioned by God and been given spiritual authority for leadership that is more far-reaching in scope than the authority that every believer has in Christ. Jesus is the perfect example of the 5-fold Office Gifts. He is the Apostle, the Prophet, the Evangelist, the Pastor/Shepherd, and the Teacher.

Manifestation Gifts or Gifts of the Holy Spirit

1 Corinthians 12:4-11, 1 Corinthians 14

These gifts are referred to as the gifts of the Holy Spirit because in 1 Cor 12:7 it states:

*But the **manifestation** of the Spirit [emphasis added] is given to each one for the profit of all.*

The word translated "manifestation" is the Greek word phanerosis, and is from a root word meaning "to make apparent"[36] or make evident. It also means "exhibition or bestowment."[37] So the gifts listed in this passage give visible evidence of the activity of the Holy Spirit.

The classical, Pentecostal teaching explains that these gifts are not heightened natural abilities, or enhancements of natural talent, they are supernatural abilities, endowments or gifts, bestowed on a person by the Holy Spirit. They are distributed to each person as the Spirit wills (1 Cor. 12:11).

The Holy Spirit bestows the gifts to whom He wills as the occasion recommends from the divine viewpoint.[38]

In other words, as the Spirit sees the need in the particular situation or setting, He gives the appropriate gift to the person who is open to receive and exercise the gift so that everyone benefits (for the profit of all).

Harold Horton, one of England's Pentecostal pioneers, expresses God's purpose in giving these spiritual gifts:

God has designed in these heavenly endowments instruments for the revelation of His will, for the building up of His church, for the inspiration of His worshippers, for the amelioration (betterment) of the distressed, for the frustration of the plans of the adversary, and for the irresistible furtherance of the glorious affairs of the glorious kingdom of His ever-glorious Son.[39]

The chapters in 1 Corinthians that deal with the gifts of the Holy Spirit are bookends to chapter 13: Paul's teaching on love. That tells us that these gifts, as well as those listed in Romans 12 and Ephesians 4, should always be exercised in the context of love. Without love, Paul says, the incredible gifts we may have profit us nothing (1 Cor. 13:3).

Love for God and His Body must be the motivating force behind using the gifts and abilities He has given us. Without His love for us, we have nothing to give. Without His love in us, whatever we give would be empty...like sounding brass or a clanging cymbal (1 Cor 13:1).

Conclusion

As you discover gifting "threads" that your Heavenly Father has woven into your being, you will realize that you may have more than one gift that is predominant in your life. You are a unique combination of gifts, personalities, and abilities, lovingly knit and woven together into a wonderful package called YOU! (Psalm 139) You and I may have the same gift, but it will be expressed differently through each of us.

When each of us is functioning in the gifting that God has given us, the tapestry of our individual lives becomes more apparent and the design God has imprinted upon us comes more into focus. We see our lives from His perspective – a beautiful tapestry – a work of art – created by the Master Weaver.

Knowing your identity in God is not an end in and of itself. It will help you to grow in your relationship with God and bring healing to the places of brokenness in your life. Your relationships with others will become stronger and healthier as you embrace and enjoy who God made you to be. But the importance of knowing your identity is in being able to take the place God designed for you as part of HIS SELF-PORTRAIT, so that His image can be expressed in the earth and His kingdom may be advanced.

Let's Talk About It

1.   Which of the Motivational Gifts do you most identify with? Share an example of how the gift(s) are expressed in a particular situation in your life.
2.   In what ways will knowing your gifting help you to understand and accept others who are gifted differently?
3.   What Potential Pitfalls of your gift do you feel prone to? Share ways that you can overcome them and strengthen your gift at the same time.

At Home This Week

Using a concordance, look up the word "gift" or "gifts" in the New Testament. Make note of the different Greek words and their meaning. Ask the Holy Spirit to bring understanding and revelation to your heart concerning His gifts in you.

Truth to Embrace

1.   All of these gifts, while diverse, are given by one Spirit. They come from the greatest gift – the Holy Spirit – and are visible evidence of His presence and activity in a believer's life.
2.   Part of the equipping work of these gifts is to help believers identify their personal gifting and understand how that fits with others, so that the body is …joined and knit together by what every joint supplies, according to the effective working by which every part does its share, causes growth of the body for the edifying of itself in love (Eph 4:16).
3.   When each of us is functioning in the gifting that God has given us, the tapestry of our individual lives becomes more apparent and the design God has imprinted upon us comes more into focus. We see our lives from His perspective – a beautiful tapestry – a work of art – created by the Master Weaver.

9

Divine Imprint

Remember the mirrors I mentioned in chapter 3? In this chapter, we want to look into the mirror of God's Word to discover our true identity in God. Let's go back to our text in Isaiah 62. You remember that in speaking to Jerusalem, God said He would give her a new name, no longer Forsaken and Desolate.

Hephzibah and Beulah
    Isaiah 62:4b-5
    (4b) But you shall be called Hephzibah,
    and your land Beulah;
    For the LORD delights in you,
    And your land shall be married.
    (5) For as a young man marries a virgin,
    So shall your sons marry you;
    And as the bridegroom rejoices
    over the bride,
    So shall your God rejoice over you.

> He is bringing us into a good land where we are more than enough to bring forth what is on His heart.

Hephzibah and Beulah. Interesting names with great significance.

Hephzibah means *my delight is in her*.[40] It is derived from a root word meaning something valuable, desirable.[41] It's a name that expresses love and security and speaks of favor. Listen to what the word, "delight," (*chafets* in the Hebrew) means: very attractive, to be favorably disposed towards, to cherish, to be bent or inclined toward, to take pleasure in. Those words describe how God feels about us.

Beulah is a name that means *married*.[42] Married to the Lord! He likens His joy and delight in Jerusalem to that of the bridegroom rejoicing over his bride. Marriage in the context of the time had the connotation of protection for the woman, a place of safety, and also spoke of fruitfulness.

New Name, New Identity

In changing Jerusalem's name from Forsaken and Desolate to Hephzibah and Beulah, the Lord is also giving her a new identity. No longer will she live under names of reproach and shame; rather, the Lord is bestowing upon her names of honor and favor. He is calling her out of the captivity of the past that was filled with rejection and barrenness, into an understanding of who she truly is – His bride, cherished, protected, and fruitful.

And so the Lord speaks to us!

I believe He is saying to us, individually and corporately, just as He said to His Son, *You are My beloved, on YOU My favor rests [emphasis added]* (Luke 3:22 The Jerusalem Bible). He is bringing us out of the brokenness, rejection, and pain of the past, unraveling and undoing the tangled, discolored, and broken threads the enemy has woven into our lives.

He is bringing us into a good land where we are more than enough to bring forth what is on His heart.

Deuteronomy 8:7-9

*(7) For the LORD your God is bringing you into a good land, a land of brooks of water, of fountains and springs, that flow out of valleys and hills; (8) a land of wheat and barley, of vines and fig trees and pomegranates, a land of olive oil and honey; (9) a land in which you will eat bread without scarcity, in which **you will lack nothing...;** [emphasis added]*

The "good land" is knowing that our value is based on 3 things:

- We are created by God, in His image
- We are chosen by God
- We are beloved of God.

Created by God, In His Image

We know that we all are made in God's image (Genesis 1:26), but did you know that He had a plan for you in mind before He ever said, "Let there be light" (Ephesians 1:4)?

Did you know that He had a hand in fashioning you, forming you, while you were still in your mother's womb (Psalm 119:73, 33:15)? He was involved in your life before you ever were!

Henri Nouwen puts it this way:

From all eternity, long before you were born and became a part of history, you existed in God's heart. Long before your parents admired you or your friends acknowledged your gifts, or your teachers, colleagues and employers encouraged you, you were already" chosen." The eyes of love had seen you as precious, as of infinite beauty, as of eternal value.[43]

He knows you intimately... and He loves you immensely

His Tapestry

I mentioned in the introduction that we are each a part of the tapestry of His self-portrait, and that He is also creating a unique tapestry in our individual lives. Ephesians 2:10 tells us that

We are His workmanship, created in Christ Jesus for good works...

"Workmanship" in the original Greek is the word "poiema" and means a product, i.e. fabric[44] and refers to that which is made by God. We truly are His tapestry!

Nowhere in Scripture do we see so clearly the intimacy with which God is involved in our creation as in Psalm 139:13-16.

If you are familiar with this passage, allow the Holy Spirit to bring fresh revelation to your heart.

Psalm 139:13

For You formed my inward parts;
You covered me in my mother's womb.

God created you and formed you while you were in your mother's womb. The word "covered" is better translated "interwoven." In the physical sense, it speaks of the white bones, red arteries, blue veins all woven together, like a tapestry!

The same thought is repeated in verse 15:

My frame was not hidden from You,

When I was made in secret,

And skillfully wrought in the lowest parts of the earth.

"Frame" refers to the bones, and "wrought" means embroidered with many colors. Earth is a metaphor for the womb. This means you were "woven" by God – physically, spiritually, emotionally, with all the gifts and talents He designed just for you while you were yet in your mother's womb.

Psalm 139:16

Your eyes saw my substance, being yet unformed.

And in Your book they all were written,

The days fashioned for me,

When as yet there were none of them.

"Substance…unformed" is language that pictures clay that has not yet been formed into a pot, or a skein of thread that is not yet unrolled or woven.[45] God saw you before you looked like you! Have you ever seen a needlepoint picture before any of the stitches have been done? There is usually a pattern, or design, stamped on a piece of fabric. You follow the pattern as you begin to stitch with needle and thread. That's the picture of your "unformed substance."

God had a design for you before your first day and has been weaving a tapestry of your life ever since. In His book, He wrote down all the days of your life, all the events you would experience, all the pain and all the joy that would make up your life, before you had lived even one day. Even though some of the stitches were not of His making, He saw…He knew…and He loved. He knows you intimately and He loves you immensely.

Fearfully and Wonderfully Made

Psalm 139:14

I will praise You, for I am fearfully and
wonderfully made;
Marvelous are Your works,
And that my soul knows very well.

You are fearfully and wonderfully made! "Fearfully" doesn't mean afraid, rather, it means with respect or awe.[46] God took great care in creating you. You were not without forethought. You were not an afterthought. Your presence here on earth was not an accident. There are no accidents in God.

I mentioned my grandson Zach earlier. He is a child some might call an "accident" because he was born out of wedlock. But I remember my daughter writing something so touching and profound in his baby book while she was still carrying him in her womb. To her yet-unborn son she wrote: "Some would say you were an unplanned pregnancy. That is not true. You just weren't planned by me."

This precious little boy is now a young man. There's not space enough to share with you the untold joy and love he has brought to my daughter and our entire family. You see, he was planned by his heavenly Father and he is here by design.

"Wonderfully" – to distinguish, to put a difference between, recognizable, to show marvelous.[47] God made you distinct, unique from any other person in the world. Brothers and sisters, even twins, are not exactly the same. God gives each one of us special DNA that makes us different from anyone else. In natural terms, we think of ourselves as being a composite of two – mother and father. In reality, we are a combination of three – mother, father, and heavenly Father! A part of your heavenly Father is woven into your very being. He puts His "designer signature" on you. You're not a Versace original, or a Calvin Klein or an L.A. Gear; you are a G.A.O. – God Almighty Original!

The Word Heals

This scripture (Psalm 139:14) brought revelation and healing to my own life many years ago. I shared in chapter 4 that my father was absent while I was growing up, even though he was physically in the home until I was 12. The Lord revealed to me that, while it took both my mother and father to bring me into the world, I only identified with my mother due to the lack of relationship with my father. Because of that, it was as if a part of my identity was missing, hence, the image of myself with no face, unrecognizable. I wondered, why the face?

> He not only had a hand in your creation, He has your picture imprinted on His hands.

Then I realized that it's the face that instantly distinguishes one person from another. When I read that I was "wonderfully made," it was the voice of my Father telling me: "You are recognizable, distinguishable, special. You have always been recognizable to Me. The feeling you had as a child was wrong. You have always been special to Me!" What healing that brought to my heart.

About the same time, I read an illustration of how God feels about us that touched my heart. It said, in heaven, God carries around a picture of us in His hand and shows it to everyone. "Look!" He cries out, "This is my daughter. Isn't she wonderful?" He gently touches the picture as He speaks. "I can hardly wait to see her face-to-face!"[48]

The Bible says it this way: *Behold, I have indelibly imprinted (tattooed) a picture of you on the palm of each of My hands* (Isaiah 49:16 Amplified).

God loves you so much, He not only had a hand in your creation, He has your picture imprinted on His hands!

Chosen by God

Paul said: *...he chose us in Him before the foundation of the world* (Eph 1:4)

The Amplified Bible says it this way:

4 Even as [in His love] He chose us [actually picked us out for Himself as His own] in Christ before the foundation of the world, that we should be holy (consecrated and set apart for Him) and blameless in His sight, even above reproach, before Him in love.

5 For He foreordained us (destined us, planned in love for us) to be adopted (revealed) as His own children through Jesus Christ, in accordance with the purpose of His will [because it pleased Him and was His kind intent]...

Jesus said: *You did not choose me, but I chose you and appointed you that you should go and bear fruit (John 15:16)*

Peter, quoting the OT said: *You are a chosen generation, a royal priesthood, a holy nation, His own special people* (1 Peter 2:9)

The problem is that when we hear "chosen" we think of being picked for a team, like when we were young. Chosen implies good...not chosen implies bad. It means some are left out. What if I'm the one left out?

But it's not that way with God! In God's economy, to be chosen doesn't mean others are rejected. In God's economy, there is no competition or comparison in being chosen. In God's economy, chosenness is a decision made from His compassionate and loving heart. God's capacity is such that chosenness with Him is all inclusive – no one is left out.

Each one of us is chosen!

The word "chosen" is interesting in the original language. It's the word *eklegomai*. It means to lay forth in a systematic way.[49] I think of Lego toys...laying out blocks in a systematic way to build something!

Before God ever said "Let there be light," He chose you, and began to systematically lay forth His design, His plan and His purpose for your life! That gives your life immense value and worth!

Beloved of God

God chose us, and made us, and He also loves us greatly. An assembly-line worker "makes" a product in the factory, but it doesn't mean he loves what he made. But God does. God's very nature is love (1 John 3:7-8). His love for us is not founded in who we are but in who HE is. That is why our behavior is not the criterion for receiving His love.

Jesus admonished His disciples to love their enemies as well as their neighbors, so as to be like their Father in heaven (Matthew 5:43-48). He says that God sends the sun to rise on the evil and on the good, and sends rain to the just and unjust.

Just as it is the nature of the sun to shine, both on the evil and the good, so it is God's nature to love. He loved us long before we ever knew Him (1 John 4:9-10), and while we were still sinners, He sent His Son to die for us that we might know His love (Romans 5:8). The high cost the Father paid to make us His own – the Blood of His Son – gives us a value that cannot compare to anything the world has to offer. He so loved the world that He gave. Oh that our hearts would comprehend the magnitude of that love!

Brennan Manning says it powerfully:

Living in the awareness of our belovedness is the axis around which the Christian life revolves. Being the beloved is our identity, the core of our existence.

In solitary silence we listen with great attentiveness to the voice that calls us the beloved. God speaks to the deepest strata of our souls, into our self-hatred and shame, our narcissism, and takes us through the night into the daylight of His truth: "Do not be afraid, for I have redeemed you; I have called you by your name, you are mine. You are precious in my eyes, because you are honored and I love you...the mountains may depart, the hills be shaken, but my love for you will never leave you and my covenant of peace with you will never be shaken" (Isaiah 43:1, 4; 54:10).

Let us pause here. It is God who has called us by name.

The God beside whose beauty the Grand Canyon is only a shadow, has called us beloved.

The God beside whose power the nuclear bomb is nothing, has tender feelings for us....

Define yourself radically as one beloved by God. This is the true self. Every other identity is illusion.[50]

Ephesians 3:20 says, *Now to Him who is able to do exceedingly abundantly above all that we ask or think, according to the power that works in us.* It's a verse we often quote when petitioning the Lord in prayer. But have you ever considered the context in which this verse appears? In the Amplified Bible, Ephesians 3:17-19, reads:

> Our value is not in what we do or how well we function; rather, our value lies in who our Maker is.

(17) May Christ through your faith [actually] dwell – settle down, abide, make His permanent home – in your hearts! May you be rooted deep in love and founded securely on love,

(18) That you may have the power and be strong to apprehend and grasp with all the saints (God's devoted people, the experience of that love) what is the breadth and length and height and depth [of it];

(19) [That you may really come] to know – practically, through experience for yourselves – the love of Christ, which far surpasses mere knowledge (without experience); that you may be filled (through all your being) unto all the fullness of God – [that is] may have the richest measure of the divine Presence, and become a body wholly filled and flooded with God Himself!

This entire passage is speaking of knowing the love of God. When we then come to verse 20, it is a cry that God would do over and above what we could ask or think in revealing His love to us! That is the prayer of my heart, that God would divinely reveal to you, the immensity of His love and the incredible value and identity you have in Him!

The Song of Solomon is a beautiful book that gives us a

glimpse of the Bridegroom's heart for His Bride. One verse in particular reveals the effect that we, His beloved, have on Him.

Song of Solomon 4:9

> *You have ravished my heart,*
> *My sister, my spouse;*
> *You have ravished my heart*
> *With one look of your eyes,*
> *With one link of your necklace.*

The word "ravished" is the key. This Hebrew word has several meanings, the most significant of which is "to beat faster."[51] What He is saying is that when we just lift our eyes to Him in love, glance at Him, His heart beats faster! Or in other words, one look from us makes His heart skip a beat! It is awesome to realize that Jesus loves us that much.

Our Incredible Value

The story is told of a man who loved gems. He went to a gem show one day and walked up and down the aisles perusing all the stones available for sale. Some were very costly. Others went for pennies.

He stopped at one booth and picked up a rather large, blue-violet stone. Compared with the others on display, it was not particularly pretty. He looked at the stone, then at the price: $15.

He said to the owner: "You want $15 for this stone?"

"Well," replied the owner, "It isn't as pretty as the others, so I'll give it to you for $10."

The man took his wallet from his back pocket, hands trembling, and gave the merchant a $10 bill. As he walked away, he couldn't believe his good fortune. You see, the unattractive gem was actually a 1,905-carat natural star sapphire, appraised at 2.28 million dollars!

It took the lover of gems to recognize the value of the stone. Just as it takes the Lover of our souls to recognize our true value. To the world around us and its standard, we may not seem attractive or valuable, but in God's economy, our worth is "far above rubies" (Prov 31:10), or sapphires, or diamonds.

In spite of our flaws and weaknesses, He loves us still (Psalm 103:11-14).

The Bigger Picture

The result of knowing that we are specially created by God, chosen by Him before the foundation of the world, and that we are His beloved, enables us to view ourselves differently – as altogether loveable and immensely worthwhile. Something happens when we see ourselves in that light: we begin to see the chosenness and belovedness in others. We are more accepting of their weaknesses because we've embraced our own. Jesus said that the world would know us by our love. The best way to love others is to first see our own belovedness.

Let's Talk About It

1.   The name "Hephzibah" means, His delight is in you, and "Beulah" means, married. Since your marriage to Jesus Christ (salvation), how have you felt His delight? His protection? Safety? Provision?

2.   Psalm 139 uses the word "fearful" – with respect or awe. God is saying you are awesome! Share the ways you see the awesomeness of who you are as a G.A.O. Discuss ways your relationships have become stronger and healthier as you have become more secure in your identity.

At Home This Week

*   Paraphrase Psalm 139 putting it in your own words. As you meditate on this psalm, insert your name in the verses to personalize it.
*   Read the following verses to understand further who you are in Christ.
    2 Cor. 5:17, 1 Cor. 6:19, 1 Peter 1:18-19, Gal. 3:13, 1 Cor. 1:2, Rom. 8:17, Eph. 1:13, Eph. 1:6, Col. 2:10, Rom. 8:1, Eph. 2:19, Matt. 5:13-14, 2 Cor. 5:21, 1 Peter 2:24, 2 Peter 1:4, Eph. 1:4, 1 Peter 2:9, Eph. 2:10, Deut. 32:10, Ps. 17:8, Col. 3:3, John 15:3, 9, 14-16.

Truth to Embrace

1.   He is saying to us individually and corporately, just as He said to His Son, You are My beloved, on you My favor rests (Luke 3:22).
2.   God had a design for you before your first day and has been weaving a tapestry of your life ever since.
3.   The high cost the Father paid to make us His own – the Blood of His Son – gives us a value that cannot compare to anything the world has to offer.

10

The Bride

The Portrait Completed

As I have studied Isaiah 62:1-5 and asked the Lord about the significance of His changing Jerusalem's name in relation to her identity, I felt impressed that there was something in that for us, as His people, to understand.

I sense He is changing our name as well…from the Body of Christ to the Bride of Christ. This in no way counters the biblical imagery of the body as described in 1 Corinthians 12, but I believe it is a picture of the progressive unfolding of us as His Bride. It is a season where He is bringing us out of the captivity of the past, with the distorted identity the enemy and the world have given us, into an understanding of our true identity in Him as His Bride.

> Before God does
> a new thing,
> there is usually
> a wilderness
> experience.

A natural body can be diseased in ways that causes it to function in an unhealthy manner. There are physical disorders that cause a disconnect between the brain and other parts of the body, such as limbs or organs. Results can range from involuntary movement like tremors, to atrophy of body tissue or organs. The latter condition is a wasting away or failure to grow in a normal manner, rendering the body dysfunctional.

That can be an apt picture of the Body of Christ. We have seen different parts functioning in their own understanding, doing their own thing, so to speak, without proper connection to the Head.

They are focused on their ministry, their calling, their anointing, and the outcome is a lack of unity or oneness. Dysfunction. Lack of strength. Failure to grow.

But a bride…that's a different story! She is joined to her beloved, her focus is solely on him. She is one with him.

Think with me for a moment about a bride before the wedding day. First of all, there is a time of preparation. Months before the wedding, there are many details to attend to: selecting a church, reception hall, guest list, invitations, flowers, cake, etc. During this time of making all the arrangements, the bride is more or less self-focused. It can be a time of great stress and tension. Having seen 4 daughters married, I am well acquainted with all the preparations that go into the wedding day!

I believe God has had us, His Bride, in a time of preparation, weaving us, if you will, into the tapestry of His self-portrait.

Wilderness

Preparation can feel like a wilderness. Before God does a new thing, there is usually a wilderness experience (Isaiah 43:18-19). As the tapestry takes shape, there are scissor snips and needle pokes that don't feel very good! We have been going through a cleansing and purifying as He deals with the issues of our hearts. That tends to cause us to be focused on ourselves.

Many have experienced breakings, emptyings, fire, and other testings as God has been readying His Bride. In recent years we have seen God purifying His people by exposing sin and allowing trials that are intended to bring us forth as gold.

In his book, Pray for the Peace of Jerusalem, Tom Hess states, Our degree of readiness for the wedding feast of the Lamb is often determined by our response to the trials we experience.[52]

Deeper Intimacy

Hosea 2:14 speaks to us:
Therefore, behold, I will allure her,
Will bring her into the wilderness,
And speak comfort to her.

He has allured us into the wilderness. In this reference, the wilderness is not a place of punishment, but a place of privacy, intimacy. For it states that He wants to speak to her heart, to comfort her. The Hebrew word, leb, meaning heart, is translated "comfort," and is used in this verse as an adverb, which means to speak tenderly, comfortably.[53] It is used similarly in Isaiah 40:2, Speak comfort to Jerusalem, and cry out to her, That her warfare is ended, That her iniquity is pardoned.

He has been drawing us by His Spirit for some time now, to pursue a deeper intimacy with Him. It is in that place of intimacy, in the secret place of the wilderness, that our identity is forged, personally and corporately.

John the Baptist came from years of wilderness living knowing who He was and who He wasn't. When the priests and Levites came to him to ask if he was the Christ (John 1:19-23), he didn't use the opportunity to promote his own ministry or in any way lift himself up. Rather he clearly stated that he was NOT the Christ, he was merely the voice of one crying in the wilderness. He was merely the one who prepared the way for the Messiah.

It was John, when his disciples came to him concerned that he was losing people to Jesus' ministry, who said, He must increase, but I must decrease (John 3:22-30). John was very clear about his identity. He never performed a miracle, he never healed the sick, yet Jesus said there was none born to women that was greater than John (Matt 11:11).

Paul was separated as an apostle from his mother's womb, yet in adult life became a persecutor of the church. After his Damascus road conversion (Acts 9:1-19), rather than going to Jerusalem to confer with the other apostles, he went into Arabia for 3 years

(Galatians 1:11-18). The Bible gives no account of those years, but it was probably a time of transformation for Paul – from persecutor to apostle – to prepare him for the mighty work that was before him.

The Word tells us that Jesus was led by the Spirit into the wilderness (Luke 4:1). But after the wilderness…power!

Then Jesus returned in the power of the Spirit to Galilee, and news of Him went out through all the surrounding region (Luke 4:14-15).

As I shared about my own identity journey in previous chapters, it was in the secret place that God began to deal with my heart and unravel the identity I tried to weave with such things as performance or looking to people for validation. But most importantly, it was in the place of intimate relationship with Him that He began to show me how valuable I was simply because I was His, and that He had a wonderful plan and purpose for my life.

In the wilderness, we learn dependency. We come to know Him in a way we didn't know Him before, and we find we can trust Him completely (Song 8:5).

Hope from Trouble

Hosea 2 continues:
(15) I will give her her vineyards from there,
And the Valley of Achor as a door of hope;
She shall sing there,
As in the days of her youth,
As in the day when she came up from the land of Egypt.
(16) "And it shall be, in that day,"
Says the LORD,
"That you will call Me 'My Husband,'
And no longer call Me 'My Master,'

He will give her vineyards from the wilderness – from the place of intimacy will come fruitfulness, just as a bride brings forth children. The valley of Achor would be a door of hope.

Achor means "trouble" and it was the place where Achan sinned by taking the plunder prohibited by God (Joshua 7). God makes a profound declaration in verse 15: hope would spring forth from the place where trouble or trial once was. In the midst of God's preparation of His Bride, there is hope for the future wedding feast of the Lamb. Even more pertinent for our lives today, is the hope that the church is coming into the unity and oneness of spirit as His Bride that will allow God to use us corporately to bring in the imminent harvest of souls.

Verse 15 also speaks of her coming up from the land of Egypt. What was the identity of the Israelites in Egypt? They were slaves. They were in bondage. They built the physical structures of Egypt by the sweat of their brows and the fear of man (the Egyptians).

God wants to bring us, His people, out of the captivity of the past – out of the identity distorted by the devil and the world system. He wants us to build His structure, His kingdom, not by the flesh or the fear of man, but by His Spirit. Not as slaves, but as His Bride...you will call Me 'My Husband,' and no longer call Me 'My Master.' It will not be as we strive and work that we become His Bride. Rather, it will be as we hear Him speak of His love for us that we will respond and be transformed as His Bride.

Leaving the Identity of the Past

It can be difficult to break free from the identity of the past when the beliefs we hold about ourselves are so strong. The generation of Israelites that came out of Egypt was not the same one that possessed the land, except for Joshua and Caleb.

I once heard about the way elephants are trained. It's amazing that a 10-ton fully-grown elephant can be held with the same size stake in the ground that it takes to hold a baby elephant weighing 300 pounds. Why? When they are babies, they are chained to the stake and they tug and tug, trying to pull themselves free. It may take hundreds of tugs before they realize they can't get away from that stake in the ground. Eventually, their "elephant memory" takes over and they remember for the rest of their lives that they cannot break free from the stake, and they stop trying. So, although it would just take one quick flick of the grown elephant's foot to be free, they remained chained to the stake in the ground.

We can be like that. Chained to the identity of the past, we're staked to the places where we've been told, "You're not enough…. you don't measure up…you'll never succeed." But a way has been made for us to be free! The Blood of Jesus releases us from the stakes of the past, from the distorted and misshapen identity that has held us captive. When we know and experience the Truth, His power sets us free – free to embrace our true identity.

> [Jesus] is not coming back for a Bride who yawns in His face on Sunday morning, or who has other affections
> – Bob Sorge

But we have a choice. We can decide to tug at that stake one more time, believing once and for all, what God says about us. We can choose the truth over the lie. When once we make that choice, God comes to us in His love and His power and leads us into the identity He had in mind for us all along.

No More Baals

Hosea 2:17 continues:

(17) For I will take from her mouth the names of the Baals,
And they shall be remembered by their name no more.

The names of the Baals represented false gods or idols. An idol is anything that takes the place of God in our hearts. So, all the places we look to for identity – people, positions, possession, even ministry – can become idols in our lives. We think that in them we will find value, security, love, significance…life. But God is changing that in His people in this hour. He is shifting our focus from our idols and ourselves and He is giving us eyes only for Him.

The Father is radically committed to giving His Son a bride worthy of the King. He is not coming back for a bride who yawns in His face on Sunday morning, or who has other affections. He's coming back for a bride who wants Him as much as He wants her![54]

At the Altar

Going back to the bride, we've said there was a time of preparation, but now the wedding day finally arrives. She is getting ready for the big moment! Making sure her dress is just right, her veil is set, every hair in place, make-up just so, she is still, to some degree, focused on herself. But, as she steps to the back of the church and lifts her eyes to the altar, there stands her beloved. She forgets about her gown, her veil, everything…she has eyes only for him! So it is with us. As we behold our Bridegroom, we know it's all about Him and not us!

A recent movie called The Runaway Bride offers some interesting insights related to our study. The story is about a young woman who has been to the altar three times, only to panic and run at the last minute, leaving the groom standing alone.

It is really the story of a young woman in her search of her own identity. Toward the end of the film, she has once more fallen in love and is ready for the special day. Just before the wedding, her third ex-fiancé offers some advice to the prospective bridegroom: "You've got to maintain eye contact," he says, pointing to both eyes. "Eye contact! If you lose eye contact with her, she'll break and run."

Shortly after, the bride begins to walk down the aisle. Her groom waits expectantly at the altar, eyes riveted on his lovely bride. Halfway to the altar, she hesitates, her step falters, you catch your breath thinking she's about to run again. But she smiles, regains her composure and continues toward her beloved, nearly reaching the front of the church.

Suddenly, someone snaps a photo and the flash momentarily

blinds the groom, causing him to close his eyes and blink. Eye contact is broken. A look of panic sweeps over her face as she turns on her heels and runs out of the church. (You'll have to get the video to see how it ends!)

I couldn't help thinking about the Bride of Christ as I watched. We are facing challenging times. If we don't maintain eye contact with our Bridegroom, we'll likely break and run, too. Our intimate, face-to-face relationship with the Lord is that which will sustain us as we follow Him and come to know Him and love Him more deeply.

A marriage is not made on the wedding day... that is only the beginning. A marriage is built day-by-day through a heart commitment one to another and is strengthened by both wilderness experiences and mountain-top encounters. In a similar way, a tapestry is created painstakingly stitch-by-stitch, thread-by-thread, unraveling and raveling, until the image is fully formed. We take comfort in knowing our Bridegroom is committed to perfecting His Bride, and seeing to it that there are no spots or wrinkles in our wedding gown (Ephesians 5:26-27).

Releasing His Favor

I believe we are in a season as a people when, as Isaiah 62:5 says, our Bridegroom is rejoicing over us, His Bride, and is releasing new favor upon us. Again, thinking about the natural bride on her wedding day, what happens when the strains of the Wedding March begin to play and the bride proceeds down the center aisle? The entire congregation rises and turns to face her as she walks by.

That is a picture of what the Scripture says will happen when Jerusalem's true identity is seen: *Gentiles shall see her righteousness and kings her glory* (Isaiah 62:2).

Isaiah 62:12:
And they shall call them The Holy People,
The Redeemed of the LORD;
And you shall be called Sought Out,
A City Not Forsaken.

These verses speak of favor being released upon the church, His Bride, so that the eyes of the world are turned toward the church, just as the eyes of the congregation turn toward the bride. God wants to showcase His bride to the world. However, it doesn't always come in the way we think!

Tragedy to Testimony

Remember Columbine? The events of April 20, 1999 that unfolded at Columbine High School in Littleton, Colorado, USA, were hard to believe. Twelve students and one teacher were killed and twenty-four other students were injured in the shootings. The tragedy shocked the nation. Yet, the subsequent Christian witness that came out of that tragedy was broadcast throughout the media both in the United States and around the world. One young student, Rachel Scott, died acknowledging Christ as her Lord. The eyes of the world being turned toward the church.

> Their Muslim guide acknowledged that it was not their brothers in other Muslim nations who came to their aid, it was Christians

I think of the earthquake in Turkey that devastated the industrial heartland near Istanbul on August 17, 1999. Friends of mine traveled to that nation to bring aid to those suffering in its aftermath. Their Muslim guide acknowledged that it was not their brothers in other Muslim nations who came to their aid, it was Christians. The eyes of the world being turned toward the church.

In the aftermath of the horrific events of September 11, 2001, we learned of ordinary men, strengthened by their faith, who became heroes, sacrificing their lives to save others. Todd Beamer, 32, recited Psalm 23 just before he and 3 other passengers overcame the hijackers of Flight 93. Tom Burnett, 38, told his wife via cell phone to "pray, just pray." Once again, in the midst of tragedy and heartache, the testimony of Christians have been heard and read around the world. The eyes of the world being turned toward the church.

More recently, in the wake of Hurricane Katrina in 2005, we watched as news reports revealed unprecedented destruction across Louisiana, Mississippi, and Alabama. In many areas of Louisiana and Mississippi, not a single home was standing. Homes were moved from their foundations, shattered into pieces, or simply gone. We began to hear stories about Christian organizations and churches that raised money and traveled throughout the hardest hit areas donating clothes, food, and helping to provide shelter. The love of Christ was demonstrated to thousands in practical ways, as Christians reached out to offer hope and help. The eyes of the world being turned toward the church.

> Habakkuk 1:5
> *Look among the nations and watch—*
> *Be utterly astounded!*
> *For I will work a work in your days*
> *Which you would not believe, though it were told you.*

Destiny of the Bride – The Portrait Completed

God is doing an awesome work in this hour among His people. He is changing our name from the Body of Christ to the Bride of Christ, bringing us out of a past of woundedness, slavery, and shame, into an identity and destiny as His Bride:

A Bride who is BEAUTIFUL!
A Bride who is CONFIDENT!
A Bride who is SECURE!
A Bride who is VICTORIOUS!
A Bride who is FRUITFUL!

As we come into the understanding of our incredible value and destiny in Christ, we will no longer minister out of a place of need, but from a heart that has been healed and restored. No longer desiring to satisfy an emptiness inside through the things we do, we can give of ourselves to others from a heart motive that is pure. The more we realize how much God loves us, the more our focus turns outward to touch others with His love.

In Genesis 48:20, Jacob blessed his grandsons with powerful words that became a blessing throughout Israel, not unlike the Aaronic blessing in Numbers 6:22-27.

So he blessed them that day saying, "By you Israel will bless, saying, 'My God make you as Ephraim and Manasseh!'"

The name Ephraim means, "For God has made me forget all my toil (grief, pain, anguish) and all my father's house" – in other words, the pain of the past.

Manasseh means, "For God has caused me to be fruitful in the land of my affliction."

In pronouncing this blessing, the person was asking God to cause one's negative past to be forgotten and the future to be fruitful. Just as a young bride is fruitful in bringing forth new life, so His Bride is destined to bring forth life through His purposes in the earth.

He is not interested in a church's self-centered existence. He is not looking for it to survive or merely to grow. He is looking for The Church to fill the earth with His glory, to subdue the earth and have dominion over it, to triumph over the principalities and powers, to be ready as the Bride of Christ. God is getting His Church worldwide ready for a final push towards the final mighty harvest.[55]

As He brings us out of the captivity of the past identity into our new identity in Him, we will take our place alongside one another as His Bride. Fulfilled in Him, the striving will diminish (Phil 3:3), the jockeying for position will cease (Joel 2:7-8), and we will move ahead as one to accomplish together, what we cannot do alone (Eccl 4:9-12).

Synergy

Synergy is a phenomenon that occurs when two or more parts working together create a greater influence than the sum of each of the parts. Let me give you an example. At a livestock show, the winning team of horses in a Horse Pull event pulled 5,000 pounds. The runner-up team pulled 4,000 pounds. You would expect that together they would pull 9,000 pounds. Actually, together, they pulled 13,000 pounds. That's synergy. A biblical example is Lev. 26:8:

Five of you shall chase a hundred, and a hundred of you shall put ten thousand to flight…

Think of the synergistic power released as the Bride works together to see the Bridegroom accomplish what is on His heart for the Kingdom!

Unity is the place where God commands the blessing (Psalm 133:3). The goal of being healed of the identity of the past is greater than our personal identity. It enables us to be satisfied with the stitch and color of the thread that we bring to the tapestry of God's portrait. The broader purpose of knowing our personal identity is for the sake of coming together as one, so His image can be brought forth upon the earth as the completed self-portrait He desires…the finished tapestry, the Bride.

Psalm 45:10-15
(10) Listen, O daughter,
Consider and incline your ear;
Forget your own people also, and your father's house;
(11) So the King will greatly desire your beauty;
Because He is your Lord, worship Him.
(12) And the daughter of Tyre will come with a gift;
The rich among the people will seek your favor.
(13) The royal daughter is all glorious within the palace;
Her clothing is (inter)woven with gold.
(14) She shall be brought to the King
in robes of many colors (NIV: embroidered garments);
The virgins, her companions who follow her,
shall be brought to You.

(15) With gladness and rejoicing they shall be brought;
They shall enter the King's palace.

Let's Talk About It

1. Describe a time in your life that you would define as a wilderness experience. Did it bring you into deeper intimacy with the Lord? Share how.

2. In what ways do you see yourself as a Bride approaching her wedding day? What preparations have you made?

3. Do you remember a time when you "broke eye contact" and became a Runaway Bride?

4. Share ways in which you feel BEAUTIFUL in Christ.
   CONFIDENT in Christ
   SECURE in Christ
   VICTORIOUS in Christ
   FRUITFUL in Christ

At Home This Week

Meditate on Isaiah 54, particularly the promises to the Bride:

You will expand to the right and to the left

Your descendants will inherit the nations

They will make the desolate cities inhabited

You will not be ashamed

You will not be disgraced, nor put to shame

You will forget the shame of your youth

You will not remember the reproach of your widowhood –
    bereavement, forsaken, discarded (like a divorced person)

Your Maker is your husband

Your Redeemer is the Holy One of Israel, the God of
    the whole earth

I will gather you with great mercies

I will have mercy on you with everlasting kindness

I swear – I will not be angry with you, rebuke you

Though the mountains depart, hills be removed,

MY KINDNESS WILL NOT DEPART FROM YOU
My covenant of PEACE will not be removed

Peace is used 250 times in Old Testament and is not just absence of strife. The word, "peace" encompasses all of the following elements:

Completeness	Safety	Perfectness – maturity
Wholeness	Soundness	Fullness
Health	Tranquility	Rest
Welfare	Prosperity	Harmony
Contentment	Absence of agitation or discord	

More than the absence of war and conflict, it is the wholeness for which the entire human race seeks. That is His promise to His Bride! That is our identity and destiny as His Bride!

Receive these promises into your heart as you begin to walk in your true identity in Christ!

 Truth to Embrace

1.   I believe God has had us, His Bride, in a time of preparation, weaving us, if you will, into the tapestry of His self-portrait.

2.   He has been drawing us by His Spirit for some time now, to pursue a deeper intimacy with Him. It is in that place of intimacy, in the secret place of the wilderness, that our identity is forged, personally and corporately.

3.   The broader purpose of knowing our personal identity is for the sake of coming together as one, so His image can be brought forth upon the earth as the completed self-portrait He desires…the finished tapestry, the Bride.

Epilogue

Perhaps as you look over your life, it seems all you see is the underside of the tapestry with its knots, missed stitches, frayed ends, and threads that seem to go nowhere. Maybe you feel your tapestry is far from a work of art.

I want to assure you that, although you see only the underside right now, your Bridegroom's vantage point from above allows Him to see the completed tapestry, and it is altogether lovely in His sight.

We are all in process. For some the process has just begun. It can be uncomfortable, even painful, when God begins to unravel and snip away the threads the enemy has sewn into our lives.

There must be a commitment to stay with the process until God has completed the work and you begin to see the beautiful pattern and purpose of your life start to emerge. God had a "finished product" in mind when He created you – He sees you in the fullness of the identity He intended when He knit you together in your mother's womb. He is committed to finishing what He started:

Philippians 1:6

Being confident of this very thing, that He who has begun a good work in you will complete it until the day of Jesus Christ;

That means that even in those times when you want to "break and run," He is right there, running alongside you, calling you back to Himself so He can pour His unconditional love upon you day by day.

Psalms 138:7-8

(7) Though I walk in the midst of trouble, You will revive me;
You will stretch out Your hand
Against the wrath of my enemies,
And Your right hand will save me.
(8) The LORD will perfect that which concerns me;
Your mercy, O LORD, endures forever;
Do not forsake the works of Your hands.

These verses speak to us as we are in the midst of the process. As we yield to the work of His Spirit in our lives, difficult though it may be, yet he will revive us. He will perfect that which concerns me: that is, He will continue to work out His purposes in our lives until we come into the fullness of who He created us to be. He wraps His loving purposes around all the sins, failures, and hurts of our lives and changes them. His grace is the enabling power of the Holy Spirit to transform us from the distorted identity of the past, to our true identity as His Bride.

THE PLAN OF THE MASTER WEAVER

Our lives are but fine weavings
That God and we prepare,
Each life becomes a fabric planned
And fashioned in His care.
We may not always see just how
The weavings intertwine,
But we must trust the Master's hand
And follow His design,
For He can view the pattern
Upon the upper side,
While we must look from underneath
And trust in Him to guide.
Sometimes a strand of sorrow
Is added to His plan,
And though it's difficult for us,
We still must understand
That it's He who fills the shuttle,
It's He who knows what's best,
So we must weave in patience
And leave to Him the rest.

Not till the loom is silent
And the shuttles cease to fly
Shall God unroll the canvas
And explain the reason why –
The dark threads are as needed
In the Weaver's skillful hand
As the threads of gold and silver
In the pattern He has planned.

Author Unknown

In closing…

My prayer is that through this book you have been encouraged to see and appreciate the wonderful and unique tapestry that God is weaving of your life…your true identity! You truly are a work of art! I pray, too, that you've caught a glimpse of the awesome self-portrait God is creating as each of us embraces our part in His design. May the eyes of the world see His Bride as never before!

ENDNOTES

Chapter 1

1 Max Lucado, The Applause of Heaven, (Word Publishing, 1990), pgs. 170-171.

2 Spirit Filled Life Bible, (Thomas Nelson Publishers, 1991).

3 Vine's Expository Dictionary of Biblical Words, (Thomas Nelson Publishers, 1985), pg.298.

4 The Online Bible Thayer's Greek Lexicon and Brown Driver & Briggs Hebrew Lexicon, (Woodside Bible Fellowship, Ontario, Canada, 1993). Licensed from the Institute for Creation Research.

5 Biblesoft's New Exhaustive Strong's Numbers and Concordance with Expanded Greek-Hebrew Dictionary, (Biblesoft and International Bible Translators, Inc, 1994).

Chapter 2

6 Janet Burkitt, "Hello, my new name is…," The Seattle Times, January 24, 2000, pg. E-1.

Chapter 3

7 Adam Clarke's Commentary, Electronic Database, (Biblesoft, 1996).

Chapter 4

8 George Barna, The Barna Update. Retrieved 5.21.07 from barna.org: http://www.barna.org

9 Ibid.

10 Marie Powers, Shame, Thief of Intimacy, (Gospel Light, 1998), pg. 26.

11 Ibid., Biblesoft Strong's

Chapter 5

12 Loren Cunningham, Why Not Women? (YWAM publishing, 2000), pg. 18.

13 Ibid. pg. 19.

14 Rick Joyner, The Morning Star Prophetic Bulletin, July 1999, pg. 7.

15 Gary Smalley, John Trent, The Blessing, (Thomas Nelson Publishers, 1986).

Chapter 6

16 Mike Bickle, adapted from The Pleasures of Loving God, (Creation House, 2000).

17 Robert S. McGee, The Search for Significance, (Word Publishing, 1985, 1990), pg. 41.

18 H. Norman Wright, A Dad Shaped Hole in My Heart, (Bethany House Publishers, 2005).

19 Life Recovery Bible, (Tyndale House Publishers, 1992) pg. 665.

20 Webster's New World Dictionary, (Simon and Schuster,1982).

[21] Julia Cameron, Vein of Gold, (Tarcher/Putnam, 1996), pg.3.

Chapter 7

[22] Henri Nouwen, Here and Now, Living in the Spirit, (The Crossroad Publishing Company, 1994), pg. 61-62.

Chapter 8

[23] Ibid., Biblesoft Strong's

[24] Ibid.

[25] Ibid.

[26] Ibid.

[27] Ibid., Vine's

[28] C. Peter Wagner, Your Spiritual Gifts Can Help Your Church Grow, (Regal Publishing, 2005), pg. 33.

[29] Ibid., Biblesoft Strong's

[30] Ibid., Thayer's

[31] Ibid., Vine's

[32] Ibid., Wagner

[33] Ibid., Vine's

[34] Ibid., Biblesoft Strong's

[35] Ibid.

[36] Ibid.

[37] Ibid.

[38] Ibid., Spirit Filled Life Bible

[39] Harold Horton, The Gifts of the Spirit, (Assemblies of God Publishing House, 1934), pg. 38

Chapter 9

[40] Ibid., Biblesoft Strong's

[41] Ibid.

[42] Ibid.

[43] Henri Nouwen, Life of the Beloved, (Crossroad Publishing Company, 1993), pg. 45.

[44] Ibid., Biblesoft Strong's

[45] Ibid., Spirit Filled Life Bible

[46] Ibid., Thayer's

[47] Ibid., Biblesoft Strong's

[48] Heather Harpham, Daddy Where Were You?, (Aglow Publications, 1991), pg. 78.

[49] Ibid., Biblesoft Strong's

[50] Brennan Manning, Abba's Child, (NavPress, 1994), pg. 57-59.

[51] Ibid., Thayer's

Chapter 10

[52] Tom Hess, Pray for the Peace of Jerusalem, (Progressive Vision International, 2000).

[53] Ibid., Vine's

[54] Bob Sorge, message at an Aglow International Conference, November 1999.

[55] Brian Mills, Time for Change, Friday Fax 2000, issue 45, November 10.

Resources for further study:

Jane Hansen Hoyt, *The Journey of a Woman*, Regal Books, 1998.

Loren Cunningham, *Why Not Women?* YWAM publishing, 2000.

Robert S. McGee, *The Search for Significance*, Word Publishing, 1985, 1990.

Henri Nouwen, *Life of the Beloved*, Crossroad Publishing Company, 1993.

Henri Nouwen, *Here and Now, Living in the Spirit*, The Crossroad Publishing Company, 1994.

(Actually, *anything* written by Henri Nouwen)

Brennan Manning, *Abba's Child*, NavPress, 1994.

Craig Hill, *The Ancient Paths*, Family Foundations Publishing, 1992.

Don & Katie Fortune, *Discover Your God-Given Gifts*, Chosen Books, 1987, 2002.

C. Peter Wagner, *Your Spiritual Gifts Can Help Your Church Grow*, Regal Publishing, 2005.

Harold Horton, *The Gifts of the Spirit*, Assemblies of God Publishing House, 1934.

Larry Randolph, *User Friendly Prophecy*, Cherith Publications, 1995.

Larry Randolph, *Spirit Talk*, MorningStar Publications, 2005.

T. Austin Sparks, *Prophetic Ministry*, Destiny Image, 2000.

About the Author
Diane M. Fink

Diane has served on the Aglow International staff since 1988 and is part of the Leadership Team at the Worldwide Headquarters. She serves as the Director of the Aglow Institute of Ministry, or AIM, an online education program which provides an accessible and affordable means for women and men to continue to grow in developing leadership skills as well deepening their personal relationship with the Lord.

An ordained minister, equipped in teaching and prophetic gifts, she also serves on Aglow's Prophetic Council. Diane brings a wealthy background of solid biblical teaching, as well as more than 30 years of experience in walking out the principles she teaches.

From retreats to conferences to small groups, she has ministered throughout the United States and in many nations overseas, seeing God faithfully drawing others to respond more fully to His love and to experience a new dimension of relationship and healing, from the inside out. Diane also enjoys serving in her local church, imparting to others and encouraging them in their gifts.

She and her husband live in Everett, Washington, and have four grown daughters and several grandchildren.

LaVergne, TN USA
20 September 2009
158389LV00003B/4/P